"Most of us are ordinary, yet God can use us in extraordinary ways. Michael Youssef reminds us of this lesson through the stories of seven biblical figures whose lives were changed by one important action—prayer. *Life-Changing Prayers* will make you rethink how and why you pray and bring you closer to God in the process."

Mark Batterson, *New York Times* bestselling
author of *The Circle Maker*;
lead pastor, National Community Church

"What liberating truth is found within the covers of this new book by Michael Youssef. God uses ordinary people to call down extraordinary results from God through the dynamic medium of prayer. That means He can actually use me . . . and you! Read it and you will agree with me that this is no ordinary book. It is passionate and penetrating, insightful and inspiring. Read it . . . and reap!"

Dr. O. S. Hawkins, president and CEO,
Guidestone Financial Resources;
author of the bestselling *Joshua Code*
and the entire Code series

"This book is addressed to ordinary people, challenging them to pray 'life-changing' prayers. Because I consider myself ordinary, I like this book. It is written for me. This book challenges a need in my heart to pray. If you consider yourself an ordinary Christian, Michael Youssef can lift your intercession to a higher level of effectiveness."

Elmer L. Towns, cofounder and vice president,
Liberty University

"Dr. Youssef's latest book is a most practical and encouraging book on prayer. I kept thinking of William Cowper's words as I read it: 'Satan trembles when he sees the weakest saint upon his knees.' After you read Michael's book, you will want to buy copies to give to every young Christian you know. And yet it will equally encourage every mature Christian as well because we all have much to learn about the mystery of prayer. This book will become a classic."

Dr. R. T. Kendall, minister,
Westminster Chapel (1977–2002)

"There's probably no more important topic for the day we live in than why and how God answers prayer. Michael Youssef's *Life-Changing Prayers* will create both inspiration and faith to find out for yourself just how great our God is!"

Jim Cymbala

LIFE-CHANGING PRAYERS

LIFE-CHANGING PRAYERS

How God Displays His Power to Ordinary People

MICHAEL YOUSSEF

BakerBooks

a division of Baker Publishing Group
Grand Rapids, Michigan

© 2018 by Leacheal, Inc.

Published by Baker Books
a division of Baker Publishing Group
PO Box 6287, Grand Rapids, MI 49516-6287
www.bakerbooks.com

Printed in the United States of America

Library of Congress Cataloging-in-Publication Data
Names: Youssef, Michael, author.
Title: Life-changing prayers : how God displays his power to ordinary people / Michael Youssef.
Description: Grand Rapids : Baker Publishing Group, 2018. | Includes bibliographical references.
Identifiers: LCCN 2018007045 | ISBN 9780801077869 (pbk.)
Subjects: LCSH: Bible—Prayers. | Bible—Criticism, interpretation, etc. | Prayer—Christianity.
Classification: LCC BS680.P64 Y68 2018 | DDC 248.3/2—dc23
LC record available at https://lccn.loc.gov/2018007045

Published in association with Don Gates of The Gates Group @ www.the-gates-group.com

18   19   20   21   22   23   24   7   6   5   4   3   2   1

I dedicate this book with heartfelt gratitude to Dolores.
Her love and commitment to the Lord Jesus and her
passion for building His kingdom around
the world is truly unparalleled.

Contents

Introduction

You and I are ordinary people.

Well, at least I'm pretty ordinary. I don't claim to have Hollywood good looks or the wealth of Bill Gates or the IQ of Einstein or the wisdom of Solomon. I'm just . . . ordinary. And, I suspect, you're probably fairly ordinary too.

And that's good news! Why? Because God loves ordinary people. Most of the heroes of the Bible were ordinary people whom God used in extraordinary ways.

But while God delights in using common, everyday people like you and me, there's one factor that made God's "ordinary heroes" stand out from the crowd: *they were people of prayer*.

Prayer changes lives, moves mountains, and alters the course of history. The people God uses, the people God chooses, are *ordinary people who pray*.

Genesis 24 contains the first recorded prayer in the Bible. It was offered by a man so ordinary that his name doesn't even appear in the chapter. We only know his name because he was briefly mentioned in Genesis 15: Eliezer of Damascus, the senior servant in Abraham's household (v. 2). We will hear this ordinary man pray for guidance from God, and his prayer will affect the course of thousands of years of history yet to come. Equally important, Eliezer shows us a trustworthy path to answered prayer.

Next we'll hear the prayer of an ordinary but godly woman named Hannah—a woman who was emotionally devastated by her inability to conceive a child. Because of her prayer of brokenness, God moved in her life and the life of the nation. The child God gave her would one day lead Israel out of the troubled time of the judges and into Israel's golden age of prophets and kings. What is the brokenness you have to set before God in prayer? God wants to bless your brokenness and turn it into healing and ministry beyond your imagining.

We'll listen as King David talks with God. Remember David's humble origins? He was a shepherd boy, a "nowhere man" from a "nowhere land" called Bethlehem, yet he was a young man who prayed. He was composing psalms—prayers to God in musical form—long before he was anointed king. We will hear him pray as he hides from those who are seeking to kill him. His prayer teaches us how to pray for mercy, justice, and deliverance and how to have confidence that God will hear and answer our prayers.

We'll reflect on the prayer of Daniel, a Jewish bureaucrat who humbly served in the administrations of a number of godless kings, from Nebuchadnezzar to Darius. When Daniel talked to God, amazing things happened. *He prayed*, and God unlocked the dreams of King Nebuchadnezzar. *He prayed*, and God sealed the jaws of hungry lions and spared his life. *He prayed*, and God unveiled thousands of years of future history. Prayer transformed this humble civil servant into an extraordinary prophet of God. We will hear Daniel pray a prayer of confession and repentance—a model prayer for all who have failed or sinned and are looking for a way back to God.

We'll hear the desperate plea of an ordinary Joe named Jonah. He is certainly the least heroic "hero" of the Bible. When God told him, "Go to Nineveh," Jonah ran in the opposite direction. If you've ever rebelled against God and suffered the consequences of sin, you'll identify with Jonah, and you'll appreciate his prayer from the belly of the fish. Jonah shows us how to connect with the heart of God, even from the depths of despair.

We'll hear the prayer of Habakkuk, an Old Testament prophet whose name is hardly a household word. But you'll enjoy getting acquainted with this ordinary man of prayer. You'll identify with him because he expresses the heartbreak of prayers that go unanswered year after year after year. Habakkuk was an ordinary man with extraordinary perseverance—and we'll see God's response to the persistent prayer life of Habakkuk. Most important of all, we will see Habakkuk grow in his prayer life, from complaining to rejoicing.

Finally, we'll hear the Magnificat of Mary, the extraordinary prayer of a sincere and faithful teenage girl. She called herself the handmaiden of the Lord, the lowliest servant of God. She was a young woman of humility, praise, and prayer, and God chose to bless every generation of humanity through her by making her the mother of the Savior of the world. All effective prayer begins with praise, and Mary, the mother of Jesus, teaches us how to sing praise to God in prayer.

Abraham Lincoln once said, "God must like common people, or he would not have made so many of them."[1] Yes,

God loves ordinary people like you and me—and once we learn to pray as these heroes of the Bible prayed, our lives and our world will never be the same.

So turn the page with me, and let's listen in on these simple, powerful, life-changing prayers.

1

ELIEZER

A Path to Answered Prayer

Genesis 24

In 1882, the American magazine *The Century* published a short story by Frank R. Stockton called "The Lady or the Tiger?" Over the years, it has become one of the most famous short stories ever written, and its title has become a common expression for describing the dilemma of being forced to make an impossible decision.

The story takes place in a land ruled by a tyrant king who judges all matters of guilt or innocence by sheer chance. He has built an arena where the public can come and see this so-called justice administered. At one end of the arena are two doors. The accused man must choose one of the two doors, right or left. Behind one door waits a lady, a lovely bride for the accused man if chance proves him innocent. Behind the other door waits a hungry tiger that will kill and devour the accused man if he makes the wrong choice.

The king has a beautiful daughter, and she falls in love with a poor young man, a commoner. The princess and the commoner carry on a secret romance. When the king learns of their romance, he is furious. His daughter is forbidden to marry a commoner.

The king orders the poor young man to stand trial in the arena and arranges to have a lovely lady behind one door and a starved tiger behind the other. His daughter, the princess, must watch these proceedings from the stands. It doesn't matter to the king whether this young man chooses the lady or the tiger. Either way, his daughter will never marry him.

As the young man enters the arena, he sees the princess up in the stands—the love of his life, the young lady he loves but can never marry. Before him are two doors. Behind one door is a horrible, bloody, painful death. Behind the other is a life he views as miserable—a lifetime of marriage to a lady he doesn't love.

Which fate does the young man choose? Death or a life of misery?

Spoiler alert!

The author doesn't tell us. The last line of the story reads: "And so I leave it with all of you: Which came out of the opened door—the lady or the tiger?" The tale ends with the mystery unresolved.

How do you solve your insoluble problems? How do you decide your impossible decisions?

How do you choose which treatment among the various options your doctor presents to you? How do you choose which college or career path you should take? How do you decide whether this person should be your marriage partner for life? How do you choose where you will live?

New York Yankees legend Yogi Berra famously offered this decision-making advice: "When you come to a fork in the road, take it."[1] Well, that advice is amusing and confusing, and not very helpful.

A wise father was reading the newspaper when his young son approached him and asked, "Dad, how do I know when God is speaking to me?" The father sighed and said, "God always speaks through your mother—listen to her."

You and I don't have to rely on the advice of Mom or Yogi Berra. We don't have to flip a coin or roll the dice or fret about what lurks behind door no. 1 or door no. 2. When we face a vexing problem or a moment of paralyzing indecision, we have a resource that's not available to those who have no faith.

We have the resource of prayer.

Over the years, I have prayed with countless people a simple prayer for decision-making wisdom: "Lord, which way should Your servant take?" That prayer is based on a prayer found in Genesis 24, the first prayer ever recorded in the Bible. (There are earlier conversations recorded between Adam and God and Abraham and God, but this is the first instance of an individual praying to God in the same way you and I pray to Him.)

It's a difficult and sobering challenge to discern the will of God for our own lives. But it's many times more difficult to try to discern God's will for someone else. Many times, people have come to me and said, "Pastor, here's my situation. What do you think God wants me to do?" You have probably had that experience yourself with a friend or loved one. It's a heavy responsibility, isn't it?

When people ask me to help them discern the mind of God on their behalf, when they ask for my counsel on a crisis they face or a decision they must make, I approach that question very deliberately and carefully. And I pray with a searching heart, "Lord, what should Your servant say? Lord, what advice should Your servant give to these people?"

Eliezer's Dilemma

In Genesis 24 we meet Abraham's chief of staff, his most senior and trusted servant, as Abraham assigns him the task of finding a wife for his son Isaac. This servant's name is Eliezer of Damascus. Abraham commissions Eliezer to go to the city of Nahor in Mesopotamia where Abraham's relatives live. There he is to find a bride for Isaac.

Eliezer's name doesn't appear in Genesis 24, but we find his name in Genesis 15:2–3, where Abraham says to God, "The one who will inherit my estate is Eliezer of Damascus. . . . You have given me no children; so a servant in my household will be my heir." The fact that Eliezer is not named in Genesis 24 suggests that he is a genuinely humble servant who does not seek to glorify himself. Eliezer is an instructive portrait of what a faithful servant of the Lord is like. He never thinks of himself. His only concern is to serve his master.

Can you imagine being in Eliezer's sandals, entrusted with the enormous responsibility of finding a wife for Isaac? Can you imagine how you would feel if your employer came to you and said, "I want you to find a wife for my son." You'd feel you were tiptoeing through a minefield.

Imagine—every time Isaac and his wife had an argument, one of them would almost certainly say, "What was Eliezer thinking when he said you and I were a match?" Or "I rue the day Eliezer ever introduced us!" Eliezer of Damascus was in an unenviable position, a lady-or-the-tiger crisis. He probably felt that he didn't dare make the wrong choice. A "good enough" woman would not be good enough. He had to succeed spectacularly. He had to bring Isaac the smartest, most capable, most diligent, most faithful, most godly, most beautiful, most sweet-natured woman in the world.

I'm sure you can identify with Eliezer. You can empathize with him. You have been at a crossroads in your life. You've stood at the fork in the road, wondering which way to go.

To make matters even more difficult for Eliezer, his master, Abraham, gave him very specific instructions as to the kind of young bride Eliezer should select for his son. A Canaanite woman would not do. Why? Because Abraham had seen the wickedness and idolatry of the women of the Canaanite tribes. He saw the way they spoke and behaved, their loose morals and spiritual depravity. God had given Abraham the covenant, the promise of a great nation of many descendants. No heir to God's covenant could be a party to the wickedness of the Canaanites.

While the main theme of this passage of Scripture is how we should pray to discern the will of God, there is a subtheme here we should take note of. That subtheme is especially important for you if you are single. Before you make a list of qualifications for the perfect wife or perfect husband, before you get caught up in the excitement of romance, before you get swept up in the emotions of romantic attraction, be sure to invest a great deal of time in prayer. Talk to God—and then listen for His answer.

Go to Him and say, "Lord, please reveal Your will to me. Show me the person You want me to spend the rest of my life with."

You may think it's risky, asking God for His will. You may not want to take that risk. You worry that God might match you with someone you aren't attracted to. For some reason, we human beings think we know better than God, or we think God wants us to be miserable. It's human nature—in fact, it's our sin nature—to distrust God's will for our lives.

But I promise you, if you seek the will of God for your marriage, you will never be sorry. When you marry the person God wants for you, the person God has designed for you, you'll know you have gotten God's best. When I was a young, single man, I fasted and prayed, "Lord, give me the wife You want for me." He led me to the best possible woman for me to love and marry. Trust God, and He will do the same for you.

When Eliezer was seeking a bride for Isaac, there was even more responsibility on his shoulders than he realized. Eliezer didn't know it, but his choice of a bride for Isaac was a decision that would affect the lineage of the Messiah, the Savior of the human race. Eliezer's choice had to be a deliberate choice, a thoughtful choice, a careful choice, and a prayerful choice. It had to be the *perfect* choice—one that God Himself had arranged, ordained, and sustained. Eliezer had to base his decision on the sovereign love and sovereign call of God.

The Holy Spirit guided the mind of Eliezer in the same way that He chose each member of the bride of Christ, the church. It's a humbling, awe-inspiring realization to know that God chose you by name before He made Adam and Eve, loved you by name before the foundation of the earth, and knew you by name before time itself existed.

We would take our salvation more seriously if we understood how tenderly God has loved us, how deliberately God has called us, how specifically God has chosen us, and how patiently God has drawn us to Himself. And I believe we would take our marriage vows more seriously if we took our salvation more seriously.

Where Did Eliezer Learn to Pray?

In the early days of my pastoral ministry, I would ask couples, "Why do you want to get married?" I have heard every reason imaginable. On one occasion soon after I entered the ministry, I asked a couple my usual question and the prospective bridegroom replied, "I want to marry her because she sure can dance!" I wondered what would happen to their marriage if he happened to meet a better dancer.

To understand the cultural context in which Eliezer lived, we need to remember that romantic customs in those days were very different from our customs today. Young men and young women didn't meet for coffee at Starbucks, go dancing at the club, go to the movies together, or meet up via the dating apps on their phones. Marriages were arranged by parents. Godly parents like Abraham chose spouses for their children based on the qualities of character, faithfulness, commitment, good upbringing, and an excellent reputation.

When Eliezer arrived at Nahor, the first thing he did was declare his utter dependence on the sovereign will of God. He immediately began to pray and seek God's direction. He asked God to make him successful in his mission on behalf of Abraham:

> "LORD, God of my master Abraham, make me successful today, and show kindness to my master Abraham. See, I am standing beside this spring, and the daughters of the townspeople are coming out to draw water. May it be that when I say to a young woman, 'Please let down your jar that I may have a drink,' and she says, 'Drink, and I'll water your camels too'—let her be the one you have chosen for your servant Isaac. By this I will know that you have shown kindness to my master."
>
> Before he had finished praying, Rebekah came out with her jar on her shoulder. She was the daughter of Bethuel son of Milkah, who was the wife of Abraham's brother Nahor. The woman was very beautiful, a virgin; no man had ever slept with her. She went down to the spring, filled her jar and came up again.
>
> The servant hurried to meet her and said, "Please give me a little water from your jar."
>
> "Drink, my lord," she said, and quickly lowered the jar to her hands and gave him a drink.
>
> After she had given him a drink, she said, "I'll draw water for your camels too, until they have had enough to drink." So she quickly emptied her jar into the trough, ran back to the well to draw more water, and drew enough for all his camels. Without saying a word, the man watched her closely to learn whether or not the LORD had made his journey successful. (Gen. 24:12–21)

Where did Eliezer of Damascus learn to pray? Where did he learn to place his trust in Yahweh's direction and leadership? Where did he learn to lean on God's wisdom and strength? He learned, of course, from the head of the household he served. He learned from Abraham himself.

If you are a father or mother, there is an important principle in this passage for you. Your children will learn to trust the Lord by watching how you trust the Lord. Your children will gain confidence in God's leadership and direction by witnessing your confidence in God. They will learn to lean on Him in confusing times when they see how you lean on Him in such times. Your children will grow to become prayer warriors by watching your prayer life.

If you are a leader in a church, business, military unit, school, sports team, government agency, or some other arena, people will learn from your example of faith in God. You might say, "But I'm not allowed to lead my office or my classroom or my team in prayer. Because of separation of church and state, I have to keep my faith to myself." That, my friend, is not true.

Even if you work in a government agency or a public school, you are allowed to openly live your faith. The First Amendment to the Constitution guarantees that "Congress shall make no law respecting an establishment of religion, or prohibiting the free exercise thereof; or abridging the freedom of speech." You cannot proselytize the students in your classroom or your coworkers on company time. But you can set a Christian example. You can read your Bible in the lunch room. You can witness to your faith on your coffee break. You can publicly share your own experiences as a Christian, just as worldly leaders, professors, and teachers talk about their experiences as atheists, Marxists, and so forth.

You have both a right and a responsibility to set a good example as a person of faith. When your coworkers, employees, students, clients, and others see how you lean on the Lord with confidence in difficult situations, you will have an influence on them. They will follow your example more readily than they will heed your words.

Eliezer watched the example of Abraham, and he followed in Abraham's footsteps. He modeled his life after the example Abraham set. Eliezer became a man of prayer just as his employer was a man of prayer. Eliezer saw that, for Abraham, prayer was not a last resort but his first impulse. Like Abraham, Eliezer began his journey with prayer, continued his journey with prayer, prevailed over obstacles with prayer, and rejoiced in prayer when his mission was accomplished.

Eliezer's quest to find a wife for Isaac began with a six-week trek across a burning desert. He went on camelback, and that gave him plenty of time to pray. He began praying in the cool of the morning, he continued praying in the heat of noontime, and he was still praying as evening fell. Eliezer prayed without ceasing. I can just imagine that, among his prayers, were phrases such as these:

"Lord, I'm dependent on You."

"Lord, You are a covenant maker and a covenant keeper."

"Lord, You have been so faithful to Your promises to my master Abraham."

"Lord, You have blessed my master Abraham, and I know You will not let me down."

"Lord, do not allow me to make a choice based in my flesh but according to the perfect will of Your Spirit."

"Lord, let it be Your choice, not mine."

"Lord, Your will not mine be done."

Eliezer also understood that prayer is no substitute for action. He prayed—but he kept traveling. He prayed—but he kept his eye on the destination. He prayed—but he kept following the map. Prayer is not an excuse for inaction or laziness. Prayer doesn't mean that we hand off our problems to God, then rest on our blessed assurance.

Prayer is work, and it's one of the tasks we must carry out to complete the mission God has given us. So we pray, and we keep working and moving toward our objective. When Nehemiah was rebuilding the walls of Jerusalem, he instructed the people to build with a trowel in one hand and a sword in the other. We are to work, we are to watch, and we are to pray.

Eliezer prayed, "Lord, God of my master Abraham, make me successful today, and show kindness to my master Abraham." He didn't ask anything for himself. He only prayed that he would be successful on behalf of, and for the sake of, his master Abraham. Eliezer has much to teach us about prayer. Our lives would be transformed if, instead of focusing on our own wants and needs in prayer, we would pray that God would make us successful for *His* sake and *His* glory.

Asking for a Sign

Abraham gave Eliezer specific directions on how he was to find a wife for Isaac. Eliezer followed these instructions to the letter. He did not vary from them in the smallest degree. He did not reinterpret those instructions. He did not make it up as he went along. He was obedient to the directions Abraham gave him.

Eliezer knew he was utterly dependent on God to reveal His will. He was utterly dependent on God to guide his steps. So he asked for a sign—evidence that he had truly found the right young woman for Isaac. Eliezer wanted to be absolutely certain he was hearing God correctly. He was, after all, a stranger in a strange land, and he didn't trust his own limited understanding. He trusted only in God's limitless wisdom. So he cast himself upon the sovereign Lord.

Eliezer proposed a simple, commonplace sign: the right woman for Isaac will be a kind and gracious woman who will voluntarily offer water not only to Eliezer but to his camels as well. If this occurs, then Eliezer will know that this is the young woman God has prepared for Isaac.

There's an expression many Christians use when referring to prayer that asks for a sign. They call it *putting out a fleece*. But putting out a fleece is not the same thing as seeking a sign as Eliezer did. The notion of putting out a fleece comes from Judges 6. Gideon wanted to know if God had selected him to save the Israelites from a coalition of Midianites, Amalekites, and other invaders from the East. So Gideon placed a wool fleece on the grain threshing floor overnight. He told God if the next morning there was dew on the fleece but the ground was dry, then he would know God had chosen him to lead the defense of Israel. The next day, Gideon squeezed the fleece and wrung a bowlful of water out of it.

Then, just to be sure, he repeated the fleece experiment, this time asking God to make the ground wet and leave the fleece dry. Again, God affirmed His decision—the next morning the fleece was dry and the ground was wet.

What was Gideon doing? He was asking God for a supernatural miracle. We should not confuse a supernatural miracle with a natural sign. A simple sign is sufficient when you want to discern God's will in any matter.

Eliezer does not ask for a miracle; he asks for a sign. He says to God, "See, I am standing beside this spring, and the daughters of the townspeople are coming out to draw water. May it be that when I say to a young woman, 'Please let down your jar that I may have a drink,' and she says, 'Drink, and I'll water your camels too'—let her be the one you have chosen for your servant Isaac. By this I will know that you have shown kindness to my master" (Gen. 24:13–14).

Eliezer didn't ask God to provide a young lady who was outwardly beautiful, with a figure like Miss Universe. He was focused on character. He sought a young woman who was willing to show hospitality to a stranger, a woman who would give of her time and energy to offer water not only to Eliezer but to his camels as well. He sought a young woman of great warmth, kindness, and generosity.

The sign Eliezer asked for was perfectly reasonable. He would ask a woman for a drink, and if she was a woman of grace and character, she would respond with kindness and compassion. If she responded, "Don't bother me! Get it yourself!" Eliezer would know she was the wrong woman. So Eliezer asked God for a sign—a very specific sign. He asked that, if the woman he spoke to was the woman Isaac should marry, she would not only give Eliezer water but also offer water to his thirsty camels.

Is it wrong to ask God for a sign when you are desperate to know which way He is leading you? No, I don't believe it's wrong, especially if we follow the example of Eliezer. He didn't ask God to cause an earthquake or send a choir of angels if this woman was the right one. He asked for a sign that was directly related to the young woman's character and to her qualifications as a wife for Isaac. His request for a sign was perfectly reasonable.

Don't hesitate to be specific in prayer. Some people say you should never pray specifically because you may be praying outside of the will of God. But the Bible contains many teachings and examples of people praying very specific prayers—and God honors those prayers. Of course, we need to be flexible when God gives us His answer. He may answer our prayer in a different manner or in a different time frame than we expect, or He may even say, "No, I have something different and better planned for you." But we should not fear to be specific when we pray.

If we pray according to God's Word, if we are obeying His instruction manual, then we will not ask for things that do not glorify God. And if we are completely trusting in the sovereign plan of God for our lives, we will not be adamant that God should do things our way. There have been many times in my life when I have prayed specifically, and God answered my prayer in a specific way. His timetable is not necessarily my timetable, and His ways are not my ways, but God loves to hear us make our requests in a specific way, in accordance with His Word and His will.

God certainly wants us to pray for family members who are outside the faith. He wants us to pray very specifically for opportunities to witness to unsaved family and friends and for the boldness to seize those opportunities when they arise. We should pray that they would have a life-changing encounter with Christ, that they would be on fire for the Lord, that they would witness to others about Him, and that God would use them in a mighty way to draw even more people to Himself. When we do, we can be assured that we are praying according to God's Word and God's will, but we should be flexible about God's timing in how He chooses to answer that prayer.

Don't ever stop praying for your unbelieving family members. You may not see God's answer during your lifetime, but that's not important. What *is* important is that God answers prayer. I have seen Him answer those kinds of prayers again and again, even years after the person who was praying so intently went to be with the Lord. I have led a number of people to Christ who were middle-aged or older, and they would say to me, "My mother prayed for me" or "My father prayed for me" or "I wish my parents were around to see this answer to their prayers."

I can tell you that I am a believer today because my own mother prayed for me with tears, and I'm grateful that she was alive to know that her prayers had been answered. You may or may not live to see the answer to your prayers for your unsaved loved one, but keep praying anyway! Keep trusting God to answer your prayers. You'll know God's answer soon enough when you are reunited with that loved one in heaven.

Bible teacher Charles Haddon Spurgeon puts it this way: "Though grace does not run in the blood, and regeneration is not of blood nor of birth, yet doth it very frequently . . . happen that God, by means of one of a household, draws the rest to himself. He calls an individual, and then uses him to be a sort of spiritual decoy to bring the rest of the family into the gospel net."[2]

Never give up praying for unsaved loved ones. If it takes years to soften their hearts, continue praying year after year after year. Persevere in prayer. One day in the presence of the

Lord Jesus, your loved ones will say, "Thank you! I'm here in heaven because you didn't give up on me—and you didn't give up on prayer."

Faithful Prayer, Unconditional Obedience

The prayer of Eliezer is an example of a principle that we see demonstrated throughout the Bible: *faithful prayer + unconditional obedience = answered prayer.*

Abraham commissioned his servant to find a wife for Isaac, and Eliezer bathed his task in prayer. He traveled the highway of obedience, and God answered Eliezer's prayer. As Eliezer says upon reaching his destination, "Praise be to the LORD, the God of my master Abraham, who has not abandoned his kindness and faithfulness to my master. As for me, the LORD has led me on the journey to the house of my master's relatives" (Gen. 24:27). Eliezer had prayed for a sign so he would recognize the bride God had prepared for the son of his master, Abraham, and then he testified that God guided his steps.

Sometimes God will speak through the Holy Spirit within us to give us guidance. We may sense a still, small voice saying to us, *This is the way—walk in it.* But when the Holy Spirit is quenched by disobedience, when the Holy Spirit is grieved by sin, we are unable to hear His voice.

Sometimes, Christians pray while living in disobedience to God's instructions. Then they wonder why their prayers are ineffective. James 5:16 tells us, "Therefore confess your sins to each other and pray for each other so that you may be healed. The prayer of a righteous person is powerful and effective." If we want God to answer our prayers, if we want

God to lead us and bless us, then we must follow His instructions. We must live obediently, according to His Word. When we are having trouble discerning the voice of God, we can ask a godly friend to help us. If that friend is truly sensitive to God's leading, they may come back to us and say, "You have been grieving the Holy Spirit. You have been quenching the Holy Spirit. You need to turn away from the sin in your life and get back into a right relationship with God. Then you'll be able to hear the voice of God speaking to you, and you'll be able to know and do God's will for your life."

God often speaks to us through the sensitive spirits of other believers. The Christian life was never meant to be lived in isolation. We cannot walk alone as Christians. We need each other in the body of Christ.

But what if you've prayed faithfully, obeyed God unconditionally, and are sure you have not quenched or grieved the Holy Spirit, yet you still can't discern the way you should go? I have been in that situation a number of times over the years, and I've found a way of praying that has guided me through many difficult decisions: I ask God to shut all the doors except one. I ask Him to leave open only one door—the door to His perfect will.

There are many ways we can seek God's will. He will not be offended when we do. God is only offended when we know His will but refuse to obey it. If you seek to discover His will for your life, make sure you're ready and willing to obey it. Many Christians seem to want to know God's will in the hope that His will aligns with theirs. They want God to rubber-stamp *their* ambitions, *their* plans, and *their* goals instead of seeking God's will first. They tell themselves they are serving God when they are really serving their own egos.

Eliezer displayed the mindset of an authentic servant. He was totally dependent on the sovereign choice of God. He knew the kind of woman who would be a worthy wife for the son of the covenant. She had to be a God-fearing woman from among Abraham's people. She had to be virtuous. She had to have a gracious, servant's heart.

If you are contemplating marriage, take careful note of Eliezer's example. He is looking for a young woman who *already has* all the qualities that Isaac's bride should have. He is not looking for a fixer-upper. He is not saying, "If I find a young woman who has 50 or 60 percent of the qualities I'm looking for, that will be close enough. Sure, she has rough edges, she's a work in progress, but Isaac can help her become more virtuous, more humble, more of a servant." No, Eliezer is looking for a young woman who *already possesses* the qualities of a godly woman with a servant's heart.

Many people go into marriage with the idea that "Oh, he'll change" or "Oh, she'll change" or (most foolish of all!) "I can change them." If there is something that bothers you about the person you're thinking of marrying, don't expect that it will change after you marry. Either be prepared to accept that annoying fault till death do you part, or don't marry that person. Marrying with the intention to "fix" the other person is a prescription for misery for you and your spouse.

Above all, don't ever marry an unbeliever, thinking you'll be able to lead that person to Christ after you are married. The Bible gives us clear warnings against being "unequally yoked"—deliberately choosing to marry an unbeliever. Any Christian who knowingly marries someone who is not a Christian is being foolish and disobedient, period, no exceptions.

Abraham understood this principle, and so did his servant Eliezer. That's why Abraham told Eliezer not to choose a Canaanite woman. The Canaanites worshiped demonic gods. Canaanite women might have been beautiful on the outside, but they did not have the beauty of holiness inside.

If you are contemplating marriage, don't expect God to overrule your foolish and disobedient decisions. Don't expect Him to cancel the natural consequences of your choices. Seek His will first, and you'll save yourself years and years of sorrow and misery. Don't try to bend God's will to fit yours.

Remember the formula for effective prayer: faithful prayer + unconditional obedience = answered prayer.

Eliezer's Prayer Confirmed

You will appreciate the generous, virtuous, godly character of Isaac's future wife, Rebekah, if you understand how God designed the camel. I know that sounds like a strange statement, but it will become clear in a moment.

The camel is one of the most amazing of all God's creatures. A thirsty camel can drink up to twenty-seven gallons of water in as little as ten minutes. You might think I'm making this up, that no creature could possibly drink that much water in such a short amount of time. Most land animals, including human beings, would die of overhydration if they tried to consume a huge amount of water at one time. But the camel has a unique ability to store water, not in its hump, as many people mistakenly think, but in its bloodstream.

The camel has oval-shaped red blood cells that are oriented in the direction of the blood flow. They can pass through even the smallest blood vessels when the camel is dehydrated and its blood becomes viscous and syrupy. When the camel can drink its fill, those blood cells expand to almost two and a half times their original volume so they can store extra water for weeks at a time.[3]

What does this little zoology lesson have to do with the virtuous character of Rebekah? Simply this: when Rebekah offered to give water to Eliezer's camels, she was committing herself to *several hours* of long, hard work. The Bible tells us that Eliezer took ten of Abraham's camels with him on his journey to the town of Nahor. Arriving in the cool of the evening, Eliezer had his camels kneel by the well outside of town as the women were coming out to draw water from the well. He stood beside the well, praying, "May it be that when I say to a young woman, 'Please let down your jar that I may have a drink,' and she says, 'Drink, and I'll water your camels too'—let her be the one you have chosen" (Gen. 24:14).

Scripture tells us that *even before Eliezer had finished praying* (v. 15), God began to answer his prayer. While he was still asking God for guidance, here came Rebekah, with a water jar perched on her shoulder. Eliezer's eyes were immediately drawn to her. There were other daughters of the townspeople coming out to draw water, but Eliezer somehow sensed that she was the one. He went straight to Rebekah and asked her for water from her jar, and she spoke the words he was hoping and praying to hear: "Drink, my lord. . . . I'll draw water for your camels too, until they have had enough to drink" (vv. 18–19).

As Eliezer watched Rebekah draw water for his camels, he knew God had answered his prayer. What did Rebekah's offer to draw water for the camels tell Eliezer about this young woman's character?

We know that a dehydrated camel can drink up to twenty-seven gallons of water at one time. Let's assume that Eliezer's camels were thirsty but not truly dehydrated. Let's say they only needed a third of the amount of water a dehydrated camel would need. A third of twenty-seven gallons is nine gallons. Ten camels times nine gallons equals ninety gallons. Rebekah's jar probably held about a gallon of water. To draw a gallon of water, she would tie a rope around the neck of the jar and lower it into the well. The jar would fill with water, then she would pull it up and pour that gallon of water into a trough for the camels. According to our conservative calculations, Rebekah had to draw that heavy jar of water out of the well and empty it into the trough *90* times. (If Eliezer's camels had been dehydrated, make that *270* times.)

Genesis 24 tells us plainly that Rebekah was beautiful, virtuous (a virgin), generous (she offered Eliezer a drink), and not afraid of hard work (she provided water to Eliezer's ten camels). As Rebekah went about the task of watering the camels, Eliezer watched her closely. Though the passage doesn't specifically describe Rebekah's demeanor, I think it's safe to assume that she went about her work pleasantly and with a smile on her lips, godly lips that sang praises to God and had never been kissed by a man.

Eliezer asked Rebekah whose daughter she was, and she replied, "I am the daughter of Bethuel, the son that Milkah bore to Nahor" (v. 24). Then Eliezer knew that she was a daughter of Abraham's people and fit the qualifications Abraham had set forth. He gave her gifts of a gold ring and gold bracelets, symbols of betrothal. Rebekah went home wearing the gold jewelry and told her family what Eliezer had said to her. Her brother Laban invited Eliezer to their home for the night. There, Eliezer enjoyed their hospitality and told Rebekah's family of his quest for a wife for Isaac.

The next morning, Eliezer arose and prepared to take Rebekah back to the house of Abraham. Rebekah's brother and mother said, "Let the young woman remain with us ten days or so; then you may go" (v. 55). But Eliezer wanted to return immediately. So they asked Rebekah if she was willing to go that day or if she wanted to wait, as her brother and mother had urged. Rebekah said, "I will go" (v. 57).

This was the ultimate confirmation that God had answered Eliezer's prayer. Without hesitation, Rebekah said she was willing to go with Eliezer. She knew this meant she might never see her family again. It meant she might never go home again. It meant she would cease to become her parents' daughter, and she would become the wife of a man she had never met. But she was willing, even eager, to go with Eliezer and become Isaac's bride.

I vividly remember a day in 1969. I was at Cairo International Airport at 3:00 in the morning, waiting to board an EgyptAir flight scheduled for 5:00 a.m. I was flying standby to Lebanon, and the flight was fully booked, with fifty people on the waiting list. Surrounded by my brothers and sisters, I waited to find out whether I would board the plane. Finally, the ticket agent called my name. The airline had only one cancellation, and had given me the one available seat.

I hugged my brothers and sisters and waved good-bye, knowing that, given the political situation in Egypt, I might never see my family again. Yet my escape from Egypt was such an unlikely circumstance that I could only give credit to a supernatural intervention by God. All that mattered to me was that I was leaving Egypt and would have an opportunity, outside the country of my birth, to study to become a minister of the gospel.

I think I have an inkling of how Rebekah felt that day. She knew she might never see her loved ones again. Yet she knew that Abraham's servant had been supernaturally guided to her, and that by going with him she was going to fulfill God's purpose for her life.

Why did Eliezer have ten camels with him for the journey? At least part of the answer is that the camels were laden with expensive gifts for Rebekah's family, especially her mother. These gifts undoubtedly helped Isaac's future mother-in-law feel better about letting her daughter go to a distant land to marry a stranger.

Will You Go?

In Genesis 24:39–40, Eliezer tells Rebekah's family about the great faith of his master, Abraham. He recounts how he had asked Abraham, "What if the woman will not come back with me?" And Abraham had replied, "The LORD, before whom I have walked faithfully, will send his angel with you and make your journey a success, so that you can get a wife for my son from my own clan and from my father's family."

Are you a parent? I hope you will see this principle in the story of Eliezer: it is never too early to pray for the angels to go ahead of you and prepare your children's future spouses.

Remember, Isaac is a symbolic type of Christ, and this means that Rebekah is a symbolic type of the church. When Rebekah's family members ask her, "Will you go with this man?" her faith wells up within her and she replies, "I will go."

The Bible does not record every word of every conversation in every narrative. With our baptized imaginations, we can imagine that there was much more to the conversation between Rebekah and her family. After she said, "I will go," they might have asked her, "Are you sure? There's a long, uncomfortable journey ahead."

"I understand. And I will go."

"Are you absolutely sure? You've never even met this man, Isaac. You don't know if your personalities are compatible. You don't know if he will be kind to you. You don't know if you will be attracted to him."

"I'm aware of all that. And I will go."

"You'd better think this over. You'll be moving to a strange land. You don't know if you'll like the weather. You don't know if you'll like the house you live in. You may not like the culture. Your neighbors might be awful people. You might not be able to make friends."

"I'll take that chance. And I will go."

Yes, there were many uncertainties in Rebekah's future. But from the way Eliezer treated her and her family, from the gifts that he brought, from the way that he talked about his master, Abraham, and his master's son, Isaac, she felt sure that her future would be bright. She didn't hesitate to say, "I will go."

That same statement of determination and commitment is made by millions of faithful believers all the time, all around the world. In 1988 I founded a ministry called Leading The Way, which is focused on reaching Muslims with the good news of Jesus Christ. Day after day, we hear of Muslim men and women who have become disillusioned with Islam. While searching for the truth, they have discovered one of our radio or satellite TV broadcasts. Their hearts and minds have been impacted by the gospel message, and they have decided to follow Christ.

These Muslims who convert to faith in Christ know that by saying yes to Jesus they may be thrown out of their homes and rejected by their families. They may lose their jobs. They may be shunned by their society. They may be hated by their former friends. Some may be persecuted by the government. They may even face an "honor beating" or "honor killing" from family members.

Nevertheless, they say, "Where Jesus leads me, I will go."

Will you receive Jesus as your Lord and Savior? "Yes, I will follow Jesus." Will you obey Him? "Yes, I will follow Jesus." Will you serve Him and love Him with all your heart? "Yes, I will follow Jesus." Will you forsake your old sins and old habits? "Yes, I will follow Jesus." Will you submit to His authority and the authority of His Word? "Yes, I will follow Jesus." Will you be faithful to Him as He has been faithful to you? "Yes, I will follow Jesus." Will you honor Him with your time and your substance? "Yes, I will follow Jesus." Will you give Him first place in your life? "Yes, I will follow Jesus."

In one sense, it's amazing that people who live in the oppressive and dangerous atmosphere of a Muslim country would have the courage and the boldness to say, "Yes, I will follow Jesus." But in another sense, when you truly understand who Jesus the bridegroom is, when you understand what a generous, kind, merciful, loving, and forgiving husband He would be, how could anyone say no to Him?

Jesus is the kind of bridegroom who loves us so much that He lavishes us with His gifts, He sacrifices His life for us, He cares about every detail of our lives, and He makes us the object of His compassion and concern. Will you go with Jesus? How can you give any other answer but "Yes, I will go."

The story is told of a soldier from Boston who lost his arms and legs in battle. He asked that a telegram be sent to the young woman he loved. The telegram informed her of his tragic wounds and released her from their engagement.

She wrote back, rejecting his offer to break their engagement. She concluded, "As long as there is enough of your body left together to hold your soul, I am yours."[4]

When Jesus chose to love you, He did not say, "I will love you only when you're good. I will love you only when you love Me back. I will love you only when you are spiritual. I will love you only when you are strong." No, He loves you all the time, even when you feel unloved and unlovable. His love for you has no limits, and He delights in answering your prayers.

The question isn't whether He loves you unconditionally. That question was settled at the cross. The question is this: Do you love Him enough to obey Him unconditionally and to go with Him wherever He calls you?

The prayer of Abraham's faithful servant Eliezer was a prayer for guidance in making a crucially important decision— a decision that would impact the lineage of our Lord and Savior, Jesus the Messiah. The example of Eliezer teaches us this all-important principle: faithful prayer + unconditional obedience = answered prayer.

When you need God's guidance, when you need answered prayer, pray with a heart of unconditional obedience. Then watch faithfully to see His answer.

2

HANNAH

A Prayer of Brokenness

1 Samuel 1:1–11

Will Rogers was a cowboy comedian, writer, and actor of the 1930s. Nicknamed "Oklahoma's Favorite Son," he made more than seventy motion pictures and wrote a popular newspaper column. He was known for his gentle but insightful political humor and once said, "I don't make jokes. I just watch the government and report the facts." He also said, "When I die, my epitaph, or whatever you call those signs on gravestones, is going to read: 'I joked about every prominent man of my time, but I never met a man I didn't like.' I am so proud of that, I can hardly wait to die so it can be carved."

In August 1935, Will Rogers was flying across Alaska with famed aviator Wiley Post, the first pilot to fly solo around the world. Rogers took his typewriter on the plane and wrote newspaper columns about their adventures in Alaska as they went. On August 15, Rogers and Post left Fairbanks, headed for Point Barrow. They encountered bad weather and landed their pontoon plane on a lagoon to get their bearings. A short time later, they took off again. As the plane lifted up off the water, the engine sputtered and died. The plane nose-dived into the lagoon, flipped over, and came to rest upside down in shallow water. Both men died on impact.

The world was stunned to hear about the death of these two beloved heroes, the daring aviator and the rope-twirling, joke-spinning cowboy. A few months later, novelist and screenwriter Rupert Hughes penned a memory of Will Rogers that appeared in newspapers across the nation. It was titled "When Will Rogers Wept."

"It was my good luck," Hughes wrote, "to hear Will Rogers make some of his most uproariously funny speeches. . . . They never failed to be side-splitting. But the occasion that haunts me unforgettably was a luncheon . . . at the Milton H. Berry Institute." The Milton H. Berry Institute cared for people who were paralyzed by injuries or illnesses such as polio.

Will Rogers spoke to the patients at a luncheon, Hughes recalled, and had "some uproarious remark for each of them whether a child, a stalwart youth, a pretty girl, an elderly man or woman. They hung on his words, smiling before he spoke and breaking into roars of laughter at his jokes. And he laughed with them." Hughes was amazed that Will Rogers could laugh and joke with people who were trapped in paralyzed bodies and "show never a sign of being touched by their sufferings."

After a while, Hughes saw Rogers take Milton Berry aside and ask where the washroom was. Berry pointed down a hallway, and Will Rogers left the room. After a few minutes,

Milton Berry went to the washroom to take a towel to Rogers. He opened the door—and found the world-famous funnyman leaning against the wall, his head in his hands, sobbing like a baby.

Berry quietly closed the door, and Will Rogers never knew that anyone had seen him weeping uncontrollably. Minutes later, Rogers returned to the luncheon with a smile on his face, laughing and joking with the patients with as much gusto as before.

Milton Berry knew that Rogers would have been embarrassed if anyone had seen him that way, completely overcome with emotion. A few months after that luncheon, Will Rogers lost his life in Alaska. Only after Rogers's death did Milton Berry tell Rupert Hughes that he had seen Will Rogers weeping in the washroom.

Hughes concluded that Will Rogers "regarded the provoking of laughter as a sacred mission. Even when his heart was breaking with pity, he kept his sorrow to himself. . . . Will Rogers was a glorious clown who forbade his tears to flow and let his heart bleed inside him lest the knowledge of his grief should mar the perfect art, the priceless medicine and relief of laughter unrestrained. There is a saintliness, a majesty in such a comedian and no memorial can be too magnificent for Will Rogers."[1]

Will Rogers lived by what I call *the paradox principle*. He understood that in order to heal others and help others, he had to be broken. To make others laugh, he had to weep. To give the gift of happiness and joy, he had to accept the burden of sorrow.

The paradox principle runs throughout Scripture, and it operates completely counter to the mindset of this dying world. The world says that if you want to succeed, you've got to claw your way to the top and trample anyone who gets in your way; the Bible says the first shall be last, the last shall be first, and the least will become great. The world says that if you want to become rich, you must look out for Number One and take whatever you want; the Bible says that to be rich you must be a servant to others and give all you can.

Perhaps the greatest paradox of all is in the realm of wholeness and brokenness. If you truly want to be whole in God's kingdom, you must be willing to be broken. There is great beauty in brokenness, and God blesses the broken spirit. You see this principle again and again throughout Scripture:

Only when Jacob was broken at Peniel—when he wrestled with the angel, and his hip was wrenched out of joint—was he clothed with power (Gen. 32).

Only when the rock at Horeb was broken by the rod of Moses did cool, refreshing water flow to quench the thirst of Israel (Exod. 17).

Only when Gideon's three hundred chosen soldiers broke their jars as a symbol of their own brokenness could the power of God be unleashed to devastate the Midianite enemy (Judg. 7).

Only when Mary broke her expensive alabaster jar to anoint the feet of Jesus could the beautiful fragrance of perfume fill the room (Luke 7; John 11).

Only when Jesus broke the five loaves of bread and two fish could they be multiplied to feed five thousand people (Matt. 14; Mark 6; Luke 9; John 6).

Only when He gave His holy and sinless body to be broken by thorns and nails and the point of the spear could healing and redemption pour forth. This is the beautiful act of brokenness that Jesus symbolized the night before He was crucified when He took bread, gave thanks, broke it, and gave it to His disciples, saying, "Take and eat; this is my body" (Matt. 26:26).

There is beauty in brokenness that the world cannot appreciate. There are blessings in brokenness that the world is incapable of comprehending.

In the first chapter of 1 Samuel, we come to a beautiful prayer of brokenness that is prayed by a woman named Hannah. Out of her prayer will come a man who will influence the course of history in a mighty way—a man who will anoint the king from whose lineage the Savior of the world will be born.

A Tale of Two Wives

The name *Hannah* means "favored" or "gracious," and she truly was a gracious, selfless, and thoughtful woman—though she didn't feel favored at all. She was inwardly broken due to her physical inability to conceive a child. Yet, as we shall see, her prayer of brokenness is a beautiful prayer that God answers in a magnificent way. God will favor this gracious woman with His grace, and He will bless her beyond her imagination.

The story of Hannah is found in the first two chapters of 1 Samuel. She is never mentioned anywhere in the Bible except in these two chapters. She is one of the two wives of Elkanah; the other wife is named Peninnah. Elkanah favors Hannah over Peninnah (perhaps because she has the sweeter, more gracious spirit), but Peninnah was able to bear children and Hannah was not. It's possible that Elkanah took Peninnah as his second wife after it became apparent that Hannah could not conceive. The Scriptures describe the tense and painful relationship between these two women:

> Year after year this man went up from his town to worship and sacrifice to the LORD Almighty at Shiloh, where Hophni and Phinehas, the two sons of Eli, were priests of the LORD. Whenever the day came for Elkanah to sacrifice, he would give portions of the meat to his wife Peninnah and to all her sons and daughters. But to Hannah he gave a double portion because he loved her, and the LORD had closed her womb. Because the LORD had closed Hannah's womb, her rival kept provoking her in order to irritate her. This went on year after year. Whenever Hannah went up to the house of the LORD, her rival provoked her till she wept and would not eat. Her husband Elkanah would say to her, "Hannah, why are you weeping? Why don't you eat? Why are you downhearted? Don't I mean more to you than ten sons?" (1 Sam. 1:3–8)

Year after year, this kind and gracious woman, Hannah, was taunted and tormented by Elkanah's second wife. And what was Elkanah's response? He tried to "fix" Hannah's sadness, but he only made the situation worse. If you are a husband, you can probably identify with Elkanah and his failed attempt to fix the problem. This is a mistake most husbands make numerous times over the course of a marriage.

Elkanah said, "Why are you downhearted? Don't I mean more to you than ten sons?" In terms of understanding his wife's suffering, he was out to lunch.

Husband, if your wife is hurting and downhearted, the last thing she wants to hear from you is how good you've been to her. She is burdened, she is sorrowing, and she needs empathy and understanding, not self-congratulatory male logic. Your attempt to fix her sorrow might make perfect sense to you. In fact, you might even think that if someone said that to you, it would perk you right up. But your wife's feelings are not your feelings, and she doesn't have the same emotional needs that you do.

What does your wife need? It varies from one woman to the next. Some women need a husband who will just be silently present with her for a while—no words, no advice, just a kind and understanding presence. Other women need a husband who will listen and nod and embrace but who will not offer advice or cheery platitudes or "solutions" to her problems.

And prayer is always appropriate. Listen to her, then pray with her, asking God to bring her comfort. Most Christian wives welcome times of prayer with their husbands. But on those rare occasions when your wife doesn't want you to pray aloud with her, cover her with silent prayer.

I also need to say a word about polygamy in the Bible—the ancient practice of having multiple wives. The Bible records the practice of polygamy but does not endorse it. The first reference to polygamy in the Bible occurs in Genesis 4, when a man named Lamech takes two wives, Adah and Zillah. Lamech, the first polygamist, is a descendant of the first murderer, Cain, and is a murderer himself who boasts about the people he has killed.

After Lamech, we see many polygamous marriages in the Old Testament, including the marriages of Abraham, Jacob, David, and Solomon. Although these heroes of the

Old Testament are never specifically condemned in Scripture for their multiple wives, their polygamous marriages are never commended, never portrayed in a positive light, and in every case without exception, these relationships cause grief and conflict for everyone concerned.

Abraham's polygamous marriage to Sarah and her maid, Hagar, resulted in bitterness and feuding. Abraham eventually turns Hagar and her son, Ishmael, out into the desert. Ishmael is the father of the Arab tribes, and the conflict between Jews and Arabs—between Isaac's offspring and Ishmael's offspring—continues to this day.

Jacob's polygamous marriage led to jealousy between his wives, Rachel and Leah, which ultimately led to Rachel's son Joseph being betrayed and sold into slavery by his jealous half brothers.

King David's polygamous marriage relationships produced a whole host of tragic consequences, including the rape of one of his daughters, Tamar, by her half brother Amnon, and Amnon's murder at the hands of Tamar's brother Absalom.

And Solomon's many wives turned his heart away from God and led him into the worship of false gods, according to 1 Kings 11. Nowhere in Scripture do you find an example of a polygamous marriage that is healthy, harmonious, and commended by God.

Here in Elkanah's polygamous marriage to Hannah and Peninnah, we see the same corrosive forces at work within the marriage relationship. Hannah is the favored and gracious wife, but Peninnah is the wife who is able to bear children. Peninnah is jealous of Hannah because their shared husband favors Hannah. So Peninnah does everything she can to make Hannah miserable.

Elkanah was a Levite, a member of the priestly tribe in Israel. Yet he had failed to be the priest of his own household. He allowed the tension and conflict between Hannah and Peninnah to fester and to disrupt his household. But the point of this story is not Elkanah and his failings. The point is Hannah and the beauty and power of her prayer of brokenness.

It's important to understand the times in which Hannah lived. This was the era of the judges, a time when the nation of Israel had no central leadership and no king. The nation was divided into semiautonomous tribes that sometimes worked together and sometimes bickered with one another. In the book of Judges, this statement occurs twice: "In those days Israel had no king; everyone did as they saw fit" (Judg. 17:6; 21:25). (The King James Version puts it this way: "In those days there was no king in Israel, but every man did that which was right in his own eyes.")

In other words, the era of the judges was a time of self-willed worldliness in the nation of Israel. The people had departed from the moral absolutes of Scripture. They viewed all religions to be of equal value. They didn't want to be told by any authority what to do; they did what they judged to be right in their own eyes. Idolatry was rampant in that era, and many Israelites adopted religious practices from the Canaanites, the Philistines, and the other pagan tribes that surrounded them. They would often pollute the worship of the one true God with pagan practices and foreign idols.

Even the priests of Israel engaged in many of these corrupt practices. That may be why Elkanah practiced polygamy, which was common among the pagan cultures that surrounded Israel.

It's possible that Elkanah married Hannah with the intention that she would be his one and only wife. Then, when she was unable to conceive a child, either Elkanah decided to take a second wife or Hannah urged him to do so (much as Sarah had urged Abraham to have relations with her maid, Hagar, so that Abraham could have children). If Hannah urged Elkanah to take a second wife, as Sarah had urged Abraham, then perhaps Hannah was being thoughtful and gracious toward her husband, but she was unwise and unrighteous in the advice she gave him. If she urged her husband to do this, then she certainly regretted it every time Peninnah mocked and ridiculed her.

Peninnah was as cruel and ungracious as Hannah was kind and thoughtful. Peninnah had a sharp tongue and a nasty disposition and used her words as weapons to pierce Hannah's heart. Her taunting must have caused Hannah to stain her pillow with tears night after night. And Hannah undoubtedly longed for peace in her own home.

You may have made mistakes in your early life that you are paying for today. You may have engaged in a relationship that has caused you untold agony ever since. Your regrets may be completely unlike the regrets that Hannah wept over. But on some level, you may identify with Hannah, with her regrets over past choices or with her brokenness over sorrows and suffering she cannot control.

Hannah's Prayer of Brokenness

We don't know for certain that Hannah urged her husband to engage in polygamy, but if she did, then she must have learned these painful lessons: we lose our joy, our peace, our contentment; we damage our relationships; and we multiply our sorrows and furnish our lives with regrets when we

act in the flesh instead of the Spirit,

judge the situation by appearances instead of by prayer,

try to improve on God's will instead of obeying it, or

try to accelerate God's timetable instead of patiently waiting for Him.

If we want to be truly happy, then we need to build our lives on a foundation of God's Word. We need to thank God that He is a God of second, third, and many more chances. We need to thank Him for His forgiveness, and we need to ask Him to overrule our foolish mistakes, our past sins, our willfulness and impatience. We need to ask Him to reach down into our brokenness and perform His miracle of repair and redemption.

Our brokenness can drive us either away from God or into His arms. Brokenness drives some people into alcoholism or drug addiction. For others, it drives them into rebellion and anger toward God. For still others, it drives them into a false religion or a godless ideology. We choose how the brokenness of the past will impact our future.

Hannah's brokenness drove her to her knees in prayer. Hannah's emotional pain drove her to the altar of God, not the bitterness of revenge and retaliation. Peninnah's taunting and bullying drove Hannah to take refuge in her prayer closet.

Someone once called the Bible "the gallery of lasting fame." God's Word shall never pass away, so those who are named in its pages are inscribed on the face of eternity itself. In this everlasting gallery of fame, this woman, Hannah, occupies a conspicuous place. She is a beautiful example of grace under fire, character tempered in the furnace of adversity, peace amid the storm, and faith under pressure. Let's listen in on her prayer:

> Once when they had finished eating and drinking in Shiloh, Hannah stood up. Now Eli the priest was sitting on his chair by the doorpost of the LORD's house. In her deep anguish Hannah prayed to the LORD, weeping bitterly. And she made a vow, saying, "LORD Almighty, if you will only look on your servant's misery and remember me, and not forget your servant but give her a son, then I will give him to the LORD for all the days of his life, and no razor will ever be used on his head." (1 Sam. 1:9–11)

We should pay close attention to several aspects of Hannah's prayer. First, we should note that this is the first prayer of a woman ever recorded in the Bible. I'm sure that there were many faithful women who prayed before Hannah and after Hannah, women whose prayers are not recorded in Scripture. And I'm sure we would be astonished at the incredible works God has done in answer to their prayers. In fact, I can tell you that I am a follower of Christ and a servant of Christ because God answered the prayers of my mother. And I can tell you that her prayers were anguished prayers, prayers of brokenness, because I, as a young man, was far from God and was breaking her heart.

The early Christian writer we know as Saint Augustine of Hippo was, in his youth, very far from God. He came to Christ because his mother, Monica, prayed daily and earnestly for his salvation. And the Wesley brothers, John and Charles, who did so much to evangelize Great Britain in the eighteenth century, were empowered and protected by the prayers of their faithful mother, Susanna Wesley.

The Siege of Weinsberg was a battle between two German feudal houses of the Holy Roman Empire, the House of Hohenstaufen and the House of Welf. The siege took place a few days before Christmas in 1140. The Hohenstaufen commander, Conrad III, became infuriated with the stubborn resistance of the Welfs and vowed to destroy their stronghold and imprison any survivors in a dungeon for the rest of their lives.

As Conrad positioned his forces for a final assault upon the enemy castle, the women of the Welfs asked for a parlay. The women negotiated with Conrad, and he granted them permission to leave the castle before the final assault. At the women's request, he allowed them to take with them whatever they could carry on their shoulders. The women would be granted safe passage out of the castle and then the assault would begin.

So the gates of the castle opened and the women emerged, carrying on their shoulders their most prized possessions— their husbands, sons, and brothers. Once the women had left, the castle was deserted. Not a single Welf man remained.

Conrad watched in amazement, then he laughed heartily. The women of the Welfs had outsmarted him, but he believed that a king should keep his word—even if he had been tricked into giving it. In Germany this incident is known today as the *Treue Weiber von Weinsberg* episode—"The Loyal Wives of Weinsberg." You can still visit the castle ruins, which are known as *Weibertreu*, "Wifely Loyalty."

In the same way that those women carried their men to safety during the siege of Weinsberg, I believe there are many women carrying many loved ones to heaven right now. And I firmly believe that, once we get to heaven, we'll be amazed to learn how many souls have arrived safely in the presence of the Lord because of the prayers of their mothers and other important women in their lives.

A second aspect of Hannah's prayer to note is that it was silent and unspoken. Her lips moved, but she made no sound. She wasn't praying to be eloquent. She was praying out of her deep anguish and brokenness. The Scriptures tell us:

> As she kept on praying to the LORD, Eli observed her mouth. Hannah was praying in her heart, and her lips were moving but her voice was not heard. Eli thought she was drunk and said to her, "How long are you going to stay drunk? Put away your wine."
>
> "Not so, my lord," Hannah replied, "I am a woman who is deeply troubled. I have not been drinking wine or beer; I was pouring out my soul to the LORD. Do not take your servant for a wicked woman; I have been praying here out of my great anguish and grief."
>
> Eli answered, "Go in peace, and may the God of Israel grant you what you have asked of him."
>
> She said, "May your servant find favor in your eyes." Then she went her way and ate something, and her face was no longer downcast. (1 Sam. 1:12–18)

Eli the priest thought Hannah was drunk. It's so easy to misjudge people. It's so easy to jump to conclusions and impugn other people's actions or motives. It's so easy to appoint ourselves as the arbiters of truth, capable of judging others and putting them in the wrong. Eli made this mistake about Hannah.

Third, as Hannah prays, she makes no attempt to draw attention to herself. Sometimes people preach entire sermons in their prayers. Under the guise of talking to God, they are really talking to the people around them, hoping they will be admired for their elaborate prayers.

Hannah was not trying to impress anyone or manipulate emotions or gain sympathy. She knew there was only One who could answer her prayer. There was only One who could meet her desperate need. There was only One who could touch her body with healing power. There was only One who could open her womb. There was only One who could do the impossible. And He is the One who hears all prayers—even prayers prayed in silence.

God understood Hannah's brokenness. He knew that her prayer expressed the sincere desire of her soul. The apostle Paul reminds us, "In the same way, the Spirit helps us in our weakness. We do not know what we ought to pray for, but the Spirit himself intercedes for us through wordless groans" (Rom. 8:26). God hears our prayers, expressed in groaning too deep for words. These are the prayers of brokenness, and He delights in answering these prayers.

Hannah's Vow

God is going to use Hannah's brokenness to bless her—and to bless the entire world in all generations. She does not even imagine that out of her lineage will come the Savior of the world.

I can testify that my most significant spiritual growth has taken place in times of brokenness. I have found that I am far better equipped to minister to people, pray for people, and empathize with people because of my valley experiences than my mountaintop experiences. The apostle Paul expressed this ancient biblical principle this way: "Praise be to the God and Father of our Lord Jesus Christ, the Father of compassion and the God of all comfort, who comforts us in all our troubles, so that we can comfort those in any trouble with the comfort we ourselves receive from God" (2 Cor. 1:3–4).

Notice that the prayer Hannah prays is also a vow. She says, "LORD Almighty, if you will only look on your servant's misery and remember me, and not forget your servant but give her a son, then I will give him to the LORD for all the days of his life, and no razor will ever be used on his head" (1 Sam. 1:11). In her prayer, Hannah asks God for a son, and in return she vows to give him back to God for His service. She promises that he will become a Nazirite and will remain a Nazirite for life.

In Bible times a Nazirite was a man who was consecrated to the service of God (Nazirite comes from the Hebrew word *nazir*, meaning "consecrated" or "set apart"). A Nazirite vowed to abstain from wine and grapes, to refrain from cutting his hair, and to refrain from ritually defiling himself by touching a corpse or a grave. In the book of Judges, Samson was consecrated as a Nazirite before he was conceived (Judg. 13:5–7), but when he grew to be a man, Samson did not keep his vows consistently.

Here in 1 Samuel, Hannah consecrates Samuel to the Lord, promising God that Samuel will keep his vows throughout his days:

Early the next morning they arose and worshiped before the LORD and then went back to their home at Ramah. Elkanah made love to his wife Hannah, and the LORD remembered her. So in the course of time Hannah became pregnant and gave birth to a son. She named him Samuel, saying, "Because I asked the LORD for him."

When her husband Elkanah went up with all his family to offer the annual sacrifice to the LORD and to fulfill his vow, Hannah did not go. She said to her husband, "After the boy is weaned, I will take him and present him before the LORD, and he will live there always."

"Do what seems best to you," her husband Elkanah told her. "Stay here until you have weaned him; only may the LORD make good his word." So the woman stayed at home and nursed her son until she had weaned him. (1 Sam. 1:19–23)

In Numbers 30:10–13 there is a provision in the Law of Moses whereby a husband may nullify a vow made by his wife if he objects to it. If the husband does not oppose the vow made by his wife, he may say nothing and the vow will be affirmed. Elkanah affirms Hannah's vow by saying, "Do what seems best to you." So Hannah kept her word, bore her son—the answer to her prayer of brokenness—and nursed him until he was weaned.

It must have broken her heart, as she nursed baby Samuel, to know that she would soon give him up to be raised away from home. But she was faithful to her promise. Her willingness to sacrifice her own joy, the joy of raising her son throughout his childhood and youth, speaks of the intensity and maturity of her faith.

You might ask, "How could a mother give up her child like that?" Hannah could only do so because she loved God and loved Samuel enough to give him up. There are countless women around the world, most of them unwed mothers, who love their children enough to give them up for adoption.

These women know they are not in a position to raise the child themselves, and they love their babies too much to sacrifice them to an abortionist. Hannah was giving her beautiful baby boy, Samuel, up for adoption. He was to be adopted by God Himself and raised by Eli, the priest of the Lord.

There is nothing wrong with making a vow to the Lord as Hannah did. But before you make such a vow, be absolutely certain that it is a vow you can keep. Many people, out of panic or desperation, make all sorts of vows to the Lord, but when the pressure is off, when the desperation has passed, they break their vow without a second thought.

God will not be mocked. Do not assume that, because God is loving and merciful, you can make empty promises to Him and there'll be no price to pay. Broken vows have serious consequences. Hannah kept her vow, and she gave her only son, Samuel, to serve the living God. Though it was painful to give him up, she never regretted keeping her promise to the Lord.

As Christian parents we are fond of citing Psalm 127:3: "Children are a gift from the LORD" (NLT). But it's not enough to merely say these words. We have to put this belief into practice by preparing our children to serve the Lord wherever they go. If children are a gift from the Lord, then we must teach our children to offer themselves to the Lord throughout their lives.

And when God answers your prayer of brokenness, don't forget to praise and thank Him. Human nature being what it is, we easily forget that God is the source of all blessings. But Hannah didn't forget. She regularly and continually gave thanks to God for answering her prayer of brokenness. She kept her vow, and the son she bore became the first of the prophets of the Bible—and a man who changed history.

The Power of Persistence in Prayer

Pierre-Auguste Renoir (1841–1919) led the development of the Impressionist style of painting. In his early fifties he was stricken with crippling rheumatoid arthritis, which eventually left his hands and right shoulder deformed. His fingers became paralyzed, yet he could still hold a brush if it was handed to him by an assistant. He continued to paint for the last twenty years of his life in spite of his intense pain and paralyzing deformities. He learned to adapt his painting techniques to his physical challenges.

One of Renoir's friends, fellow painter Henri Matisse, was amazed at his ability to endure suffering for the sake of his art. Matisse asked Renoir, "Why do you torture yourself to keep painting?"

"The pain passes," Renoir replied, "but the beauty remains."[2]

Persistence wins the battle. No battle was ever won by surrendering. I once heard about a politician who expressed his commitment to his cause with something like, "I will fight this proposition until hell freezes over—then I will start fighting on the ice." That's persistence.

The worldly view of life and the godly view of life are at odds precisely over the virtue of persistence, as these examples show:

> The world demands instant gratification. God's Word commends perseverance.
>
> The world promotes instant results. God's Word commends the long view.
>
> The world says, "Break down doors to get what you want." God's Word commends patience.

The world says, "Live for the moment." God's Word commends an eternal perspective.

Many voices in our secular, post-Christian culture tell us to demand what we want and to demand it *now*! But God's Word tells us to pray with patience and persistence.

The opposite of persistence is surrender, and if we give up on our prayer life, we can expect nothing but spiritual defeat and spiritual discouragement. There are many casualties in the Christian life, and most of them are people who did not persist in prayer. While perseverance is a Christian virtue, even non-Christians understand the value of persistence when it comes to developing a skill, learning a language, achieving a goal, or breaking a bad habit. Those who succeed are those who refuse to give up; those who succeed in the things of God are those who persist in prayer.

The Christian life is a battlefield. That's why the apostle Paul says, "For our struggle is not against flesh and blood, but against the rulers, against the authorities, against the powers of this dark world and against the spiritual forces of evil in the heavenly realms" (Eph. 6:12).

I can testify from my own spiritual battles that there is no place in which persistence is more rewarding than when we are battling on our knees in prayer. There is no battlefield in which victory is more certain than when we persistently wrestle against the powers of this dark world through prayer. There is no battlefield in the world—not Hastings, nor Waterloo, nor Gettysburg, nor Iwo Jima, nor Fallujah—which is more crucial to the outcome than the battle taking place in your prayer closet.

We have just seen this gracious and faithful woman, Hannah, win a great victory on her knees in prayer. She persisted in prayer, lived up to the meaning of her name ("gracious"), endured the taunting of her husband's other wife, and allowed her suffering to drive her deeper into the heart of God instead of toward revenge. She made a promise to God: give me a son and I will give him back to You. And she kept her promise. Her son, Samuel, blessed the whole world throughout the generations.

Five Ingredients of Hannah's Prayer

Let's take a closer look at the prayer Hannah prayed, and we'll see five ingredients in her prayer that are instructive and inspirational to us today. They are surrender, sorrow, supplication, song, and sacrifice. Let's look at each of these in turn.

Surrender

Hannah's prayer was a prayer of persistence, yet it was also a prayer of surrender, the godly kind of surrender. She refused to surrender to despair. Instead, she surrendered everything to God. Her surrender to the Lord was unconditional. She handed total ownership of her life to Him, holding nothing back. She gave God the deed to her life, the deed to everything she was and everything she owned, including the baby she had prayed to conceive.

Have you and I reached a place of spiritual maturity in which we can pray the prayer of Hannah, the prayer of absolute surrender to God? Most of us are willing to give a portion to God as long as it doesn't interfere with our "right" to live our lives as we please. We say, "Lord, I surrender this compartment of my life to You, but the rest is mine." We don't object to giving Him our leftovers, but we want to keep the best for ourselves.

When we hold back from God, when we cut back our giving to Him, we are being like the farmer in Aesop's fable about the goose that laid the golden eggs. The farmer got tired of waiting for a single golden egg per day, so he cut the goose open to get all the eggs at once. He failed to understand that the goose laid a new egg of blessing every day. By cutting open the goose, he had killed the source of daily blessing.

When we surrender everything to God, He responds by blessing us. If we hold back, we cut open the goose and cut off the blessing God wants to give us each day. When Hannah surrendered to God, she gave Him the one thing she loved more than anything else in the world—the child of her prayer of brokenness. When she surrendered everything to Him, He was able to bless her in an amazing way.

The same God who blessed Hannah and answered her prayer of brokenness still wants to bless you today. Surrender everything to Him and see how He blesses you.

Sorrow

Let's not have any illusions. Hannah's prayer of surrender to the Lord did not spare her from sorrow and pain. She continued to suffer pain from Peninnah's sharp tongue. She had a house, but not a home, not a haven of rest in peace. She had a devoted husband, but she also had a fierce and mean-spirited rival for his affection. She endured constant cruelty and perpetual taunting.

She describes herself to Eli as "a woman who is deeply troubled" (1 Sam. 1:15). In other translations, this statement sounds even more despairing: "I am a woman oppressed in spirit" (NASB) or "I am a woman of a sorrowful spirit" (NKJV) or "I am a woman with a broken heart" (CSB).

Yet, even in the midst of her sorrow, Hannah trusts the Lord. Though her womb is shut, her heart is open to God. Though her anguish is unbearable, she leans on God.

You may understand from your own experience how Hannah feels. You may be struggling with a family member, a boss, a coworker, a neighbor, or a fellow church member, someone who is cruel to you, has wounded you deeply, or has abandoned or betrayed you, and you are oppressed in spirit and brokenhearted. Remember, nothing is hidden from God's view. Someone in your life may treat you as worthless, but in God's sight you are worth more than rubies and sapphires.

It may seem that your trial is unending and your prayers are unanswered, even as your sorrows mount to the sky. Remember, you have a provider who is limitless, a protector who is all-powerful, a promise that is unchanging, and possessions that are unfading. Hannah's sorrow is deep as she prays this prayer of brokenness, but her sorrow will not last forever.

God is about to bring joy into her life.

Supplication

Supplication is the act of asking for something in an earnest and humble way. In her prayer, Hannah didn't presume to demand anything from God. She didn't feel God owed her anything. She came to Him on her knees, humbly begging and pleading for undeserved grace and mercy from her Lord.

In her sorrow, Hannah refused to give in to bitterness. She was mentally hurt, but her soul would be healed. She was emotionally battered, but her commitment was unshakable.

She was physically exhausted from the daily aggravation of the rival wife, but she was spiritually powerful. She had every reason to give up, yet she persevered in prayer.

What did she pray for? What was her supplication to God? It was nothing less than a plea that God would intervene in the laws of nature and open her womb.

I am convinced that, as the forces of secularism continue to rise in our world, we will see increasingly vicious attacks on the Christian faith. Christians will cry out for more and more supernatural intervention from God and God will answer those supplications that are prayed with persistence.

Why don't we see more miracles and supernatural interventions today? As long as Christians choose to live, for all intents and purposes, as if they were atheists, God says, "Go ahead and live by sight and not by faith. If you change your mind and decide to live by faith, I will intervene." But as we become stronger in Christ, we will see His hand moving in the world in ways we have never seen before.

Song

After baby Samuel was weaned, it was time for Hannah to give him over to the Lord, in keeping with her vow. I can imagine that she kept her baby at her breast as long as she could, wanting to keep the day of his weaning as far off as possible. But eventually, she had to accept that her little son could be nourished and cared for by others, and it was time to give him up.

So Hannah and her husband took the boy, along with animals for sacrifices, to the house of the Lord at Shiloh. After making the sacrifices prescribed in the law of Moses, they brought the boy to Eli, the High Priest, and Hannah reintroduced herself as the woman Eli had seen praying to the Lord. "I prayed for this child," the mother said, "and the LORD has granted me what I asked of him. So now I give him to the LORD. For his whole life he will be given over to the LORD."

Then Hannah sang a song to the Lord, which is recorded in the opening verses of 1 Samuel 2:

> My heart rejoices in the LORD;
>   in the LORD my horn is lifted high.
> My mouth boasts over my enemies,
>   for I delight in your deliverance.
>
> There is no one holy like the LORD;
>   there is no one besides you;
>   there is no Rock like our God.
>
> Do not keep talking so proudly
>   or let your mouth speak such arrogance,
> for the LORD is a God who knows,
>   and by him deeds are weighed.
>
> The bows of the warriors are broken,
>   but those who stumbled are armed with strength.
> Those who were full hire themselves out for food,
>   but those who were hungry are hungry no more.
> She who was barren has borne seven children,
>   but she who has had many sons pines away.
>
> The LORD brings death and makes alive;
>   he brings down to the grave and raises up.
> The LORD sends poverty and wealth;
>   he humbles and he exalts.
> He raises the poor from the dust
>   and lifts the needy from the ash heap;

he seats them with princes
   and has them inherit a throne of honor.

For the foundations of the earth are the LORD's;
   on them he has set the world.
He will guard the feet of his faithful servants,
   but the wicked will be silenced in the place of
      darkness.

It is not by strength that one prevails;
   those who oppose the LORD will be broken.
The Most High will thunder from heaven;
   the LORD will judge the ends of the earth.

He will give strength to his king
   and exalt the horn of his anointed. (vv. 1–10)

After singing this hymn to the Lord, Hannah returned with her husband to their home in Ramah, but the boy remained in Shiloh. There he ministered before the Lord and was instructed by Eli the priest.

The song of Hannah reminds us of the Magnificat, the song Mary sang after the angel told her she was carrying the Son of God in her womb. In the closing chapter of this book we will look at Mary's song and we'll see similarities between these two beautiful hymns of praise by two great women of faith.

As Christians, we love to praise the Lord. We praise Him for salvation, for blessings, for the great things He has done for us, for His kindness and mercy to us. But Hannah praises God for one of His attributes that Christians in the twenty-first century easily forget—His holiness. It takes a 100 percent–surrendered soul to sing of the holiness of the Lord. Those who praise the holiness of God stand on a higher spiritual plane than most believers. Hannah says:

> There is no one holy like the LORD;
>   there is no one besides you;
>   there is no Rock like our God. (v. 2)

A rock is a place of security—a fortress and a stronghold in times of trouble and conflict. Hannah did not seek her security in wealth, friends, or even her husband. Her only security was in the One whose stability is unshakable, whose comfort is incomparable, whose power is unconquerable, whose compassion is inexhaustible, whose shield is impenetrable, whose peace is unexplainable, and whose love is unchangeable. Her sense of security came from being safely held and hidden by the Rock, the strong tower of the Lord.

In verse 1 Hannah says, "My heart rejoices in the LORD; in the LORD my horn is lifted high." In the Bible, horns generally speak of pride and power. This imagery comes from an ox whose strength is in his horns. It's important to understand that Hannah does not use this imagery to boast of her own pride and power. Rather, she is saying that all of her pride, all of her power, is "in the Lord" alone. In other words, she has nothing to boast of in herself and everything to boast of in the Lord. It's a statement of humility and a statement of praise to the majesty and power of God. She is saying, "In my own strength, I am nothing. I can accomplish nothing. I can succeed in nothing. I could not have a child in my own strength, but I gave birth to a child by the power of God."

The Lord will always give a song of praise to the surrendered soul. He will always give a song of praise to the heart full of supplication. He will always put a song of praise on the lips of those who are 100 percent sold out to Him. God's song of praise is power to the powerless, strength to the weak, joy to the joyless, healing to the wounded soul, victory to the defeated, and a sacrifice to the Lord. That's why the Bible speaks of "a sacrifice of praise" (Heb. 13:15).

Sacrifice

Hannah made a selfless, sacrificial vow to the Lord. She told God that if He would answer her prayer for a son, she would dedicate the child to Him. And she kept her vow, though it cost her many tears. There is nothing in the world that Hannah wanted more than that baby boy, but as soon as he was weaned, she gave him back to the Lord as a living sacrifice.

The pagan nations that surrounded Israel, the Canaanites and the Philistines and others, worshiped demonic gods and idols made of brass, and these pagans would sacrifice their precious little children, slaughter them on the altar as sacrifices to their false gods. But Hannah loved little Samuel enough to give him to the Lord as a *living* sacrifice, a boy who would grow to be a great spiritual leader in Israel.

The noble and faithful sacrifice of Hannah challenges you and me. It forces us to first ask ourselves: What is the one thing I really want from the hand of the Lord? What is the one thing I want from God more than anything else in the world? We all have a desire in us. Everyone will answer this question differently. We are all individuals, and the burning desires of our souls will be different from one another.

Once we have answered this first question, then we must answer a second question: If the Lord answered my prayer and gave me the desire of my heart, would I be willing to give it back to Him?

I'm sure Hannah often went to Shiloh to visit her son, but it wasn't the same as having him at home. She didn't get to teach him his first words. She didn't get to play with him and take him on walks. She didn't get to tuck him into bed at night. She didn't get to do the things mothers love to do with their children. All of these things Hannah placed on the altar of the Lord as a sacrifice to Him.

Why do we need to sacrifice the things we love most to God? He doesn't need these things. We can't make God richer by giving these things to Him. But our sacrifices reveal the state of our hearts. God wants to know that we hold the blessings He gives us loosely, with open hands. He doesn't want us to cling to things or to people or even to our children; He wants us to cling to Him.

Hannah didn't wait until Samuel became a man to give him to the Lord. She didn't try to change the rules and redefine what giving back to the Lord really means. She didn't try to rationalize her vow and say, "I'll keep Samuel with me so I can train him and build a relationship with him. A boy needs his mother, after all. I know I made a vow to God, but God will understand if I alter the terms of that vow just a bit."

Does that kind of rationalizing sound familiar? Have you ever engaged in that kind of thinking yourself? Hannah refused to even bend her vow, much less break it. She kept her vow and sacrificed much of her motherly happiness, but as her song reveals, she held on to her deep joy in the Lord. She gave Samuel to the Lord as a baby, just weaned, to be raised as a consecrated servant of the Lord.

As Samuel grew to manhood, he was a blessing to not only his mother but also his entire generation and millions of people yet unborn. Samuel changed history. He turned the people's hearts back to the Lord. He anointed King David, the ancestor of the Lord Jesus. And that is not the end of the story.

God responded to Hannah's faithfulness and sacrifice by giving her five more children. When she kept her vow to the Lord, she had no idea that she would receive not only Samuel but also five more sons and daughters. That's how God works. That's how He responds to sacrificial praise and complete surrender.

If we truly understand God's economy, we will realize that our sacrifices are not really sacrifices at all. The Lord will always bless the fully surrendered sacrifice. God answers the prayer of brokenness, and He will not be a debtor to any man or woman. He always repays our sacrifices with an abundance of blessing.

3

DAVID

A Prayer for Mercy and Justice

Psalm 28

Some years ago, a friend asked me, "Michael, are you a shy person?"

No one had ever asked me that before. Because I'm a public speaker and I regularly appear on television, people assume I have a naturally outgoing personality. But as I confided to my friend, I'm a shy person by nature. In fact, as a boy I was so bashful that I could never look strangers in the eye. If a visitor knocked on the front door, I'd run to my room to avoid having to talk to a stranger.

I've often wondered why God chose that shy, socially awk-ward little boy and thrust him into public ministry. Why did God choose an introvert like me when there are so many extroverts to choose from? I don't know the answer to that question. I only know that God sovereignly arranged the circumstances of my early life to prod me out of my comfort zone. Against my will He dragged me from bashfulness to boldness.

Much of my shyness was due to low self-esteem. I didn't think I had any talents or abilities. At age twenty-two I took a sheet of paper and tried to make a list of my personality assets and liabilities. My list of defects and flaws was long— I needed an additional page to list them all. But my list of talents and abilities was completely blank. I couldn't think of a single gift or talent God had given me to use for His service. I saw myself as a nobody.

But I decided I would be a nobody who prayed. I said, "Lord Jesus, I know You died on the cross for my sins. You gave Your all to me, and I have nothing to give to You. My all is next to nothing, but whatever I have is Yours to use in any way You want to."

After I prayed that prayer, God began opening up possibilities and opportunities for me, and He ultimately led me to become a pastor, speaker, and author—a future I never dared to think was possible when I was that bashful, timid little boy.

I sometimes wonder if David, when he was a shepherd boy, ever thought about his future. When he was out in the fields, watching the sheep, composing his poems, and battling the occasional bear or lion, I'm sure he never imagined he would one day be king of Israel. What natural skills and talents did he possess that would equip him to lead the nation? What administrative or leadership skills did he demonstrate while sitting on a hillside, watching over his flocks? When you read his story in the Scriptures, it's clear that his father and brothers didn't see him as leadership material.

Yet God saw the makings of a king within that boy, much as a sculptor sees a masterpiece hidden within a block of marble. Perhaps the most important quality God saw in young David was his prayerfulness, which he expressed through the songs and psalms he composed from an early age. We know that even in his youth, David was skilled at playing the harp-like lyre and singing songs to the Lord because King Saul enjoyed his worship songs so much that he made David his court musician.

God told Samuel to anoint David as Israel's future king long before David demonstrated any skill or aptitude for leadership. Why did God choose this singing shepherd boy for the most important executive position in the kingdom? I don't know for sure, but I would like to offer an educated guess: *David prayed.* He sang prayerful, heartfelt songs to the Lord. I believe God looked at David's heart and saw a young man who wanted nothing more than an intimate relationship with the Lord. That was the only qualification that mattered to God.

The prophet Samuel anointed the first two kings of Israel, and those two kings were a study in contrasts. Israel's first king, Saul, was *man's* king, the king the people of Israel demanded from God in opposition to God's own advice. Israel's second king, David, was *God's* king, the one God supernaturally chose to succeed King Saul even while Saul still lived.

King David is one of the most significant figures in the Bible. A large section of the Old Testament is devoted primarily to David, from 1 Samuel 16 through the end of 2 Samuel and 1 Kings 1–2. His name is mentioned more than six hundred times throughout the Old Testament. His name appears on the first page and last page of the New Testament (Matt. 1:6 and Rev. 22:16).

In 1 Samuel 13:14 and Acts 13:22, David is called a man after God's own heart. This does not mean that David was morally perfect because he assuredly was not. But he was a man whose heart was humble, reverent, and sensitive to God's leading. After his great sin of adultery and murder, God called him to repentance through the prophet Nathan, and David responded instantly in tears and horror over his sin.

King David came from humble, ordinary circumstances. He was not born to royalty but was the son of a rancher, a common man of the common people, a "nowhere man" from a "nowhere land" called Bethlehem. He was a devoutly spiritual musician who composed most of the songs in the hymnbook of Israel, the book of Psalms. He was a simple shepherd boy. He was also the direct ancestor of the Messiah, the Lord Jesus Christ.

God prepared young David to be king by bringing this common, ordinary shepherd boy into the orbit of King Saul. Israel's first king, Saul, was a deeply troubled man—troubled in soul and spirit. Saul brought young David into the royal court to minister to his tortured soul through music. Saul also chose David to be his armor bearer, a position that gave David a closeup view of how King Saul conducted affairs of state. An armor bearer was also something of a protector and bodyguard to the king, so young David was, in a sense, King Saul's personal Secret Service agent. In this way, God trained and prepared David to one day become the king of Israel.

As a shepherd from Bethlehem, as a man of the people, as a warrior, and as king, David was a prophetic type of the coming Messiah, Jesus the Lord. We will examine one of David's many prayers in musical form—Psalm 28.

A Plea for Mercy and Justice

History has shown that successful leaders do not automatically make successful fathers. Some extremely successful and influential leaders in business, politics, the media, and even the pastorate have failed tragically as fathers. King David was one such leader.

David was a great warrior, great king, great songwriter, and great spiritual leader, yet his track record as a father was, at best, mixed. There is probably not just one factor we can point to as the reason King David experienced failure as a father. There are probably a number of reasons. As we saw in the previous chapter, polygamy—the ancient practice of marrying more than one wife—was corrosive to marital and family harmony. Polygamous marriages tended to be rife with conflict, rivalries, and bitterness.

The exact number of David's wives is unknown, but a number of his wives are mentioned by name in the Bible: Michal (daughter of King Saul), Ahinoam the Jezreelite (the mother of Amnon), Abigail the Carmelite, Maachah (the mother of Absalom and his sister Tamar), Haggith, Abital, Eglah, and Bathsheba (who had previously been the wife of Uriah the Hittite and was the mother of Solomon). The Scriptures tell us that David took other wives and concubines in addition to those who are named (2 Sam. 5:13).

The rivalries between the children of King David's wives probably led to such tragic consequences as the rape of David's daughter Tamar by her half brother Amnon (David's firstborn son) and Amnon's murder at the hands of Tamar's brother Absalom. These events grieved David deeply. Absalom, David's third (and much-beloved) son, later usurped David's throne and publicly disgraced David by having sexual relations with David's concubines. The struggle between David and Absalom tipped Israel into a civil war that forced David to flee from Absalom and ended with Absalom's violent death. Even though Absalom had mounted a coup d'état against his father, David had hoped for a reconciliation and was heartbroken over Absalom's death.

David's family was torn apart by rape, murder, rebellion, and revolution. David failed as a father, in part because of his polygamous marriages and in part because he was too busy with matters of government and war to be an involved, influential parent to his sons and daughters by various wives. He was powerful, he was successful, he was the king—but he was eventually on the run, fleeing a son who sought to take his life.

David's kingdom was torn by civil war, and his emotions were torn by his struggle with Absalom. Exiled from his family and his people, hiding from his son Absalom, a grief-stricken King David penned a heartfelt prayer, a plea for mercy and justice. It's a prayer that expresses the heart's cry of everyone who has found themselves in a desperate situation. Inspired by the Holy Spirit, David wrote the prayer of Psalm 28:

> To you, LORD, I call;
>> you are my Rock,
>> do not turn a deaf ear to me.
> For if you remain silent,
>> I will be like those who go down to the pit.

Hear my cry for mercy
    as I call to you for help,
as I lift up my hands
    toward your Most Holy Place.

Do not drag me away with the wicked,
    with those who do evil,
who speak cordially with their neighbors
    but harbor malice in their hearts.
Repay them for their deeds
    and for their evil work;
repay them for what their hands have done
    and bring back on them what they deserve.

Because they have no regard for the deeds of the
    Lord
    and what his hands have done,
he will tear them down
    and never build them up again.

Praise be to the Lord,
    for he has heard my cry for mercy.
The Lord is my strength and my shield;
    my heart trusts in him, and he helps me.
My heart leaps for joy,
    and with my song I praise him.

The Lord is the strength of his people,
    a fortress of salvation for his anointed one.
Save your people and bless your inheritance;
    be their shepherd and carry them forever.

David wrote a number of psalms like this one, psalms that Charles Haddon Spurgeon called "songs of the night."[1] These were psalms in which David's suffering and grief lent eloquence to his music. He had endured betrayal, disgrace, and hatred from the son he loved, so he went to God in prayer, pleading for mercy and an end to his unjust suffering. When he composed these lines, David was probably in the hills at Mahanaim across the Jordan, mustering his forces for battle against the rebellious army of Absalom (2 Sam. 17).

This psalm is a comforting passage to meditate on when you have been slandered, mistreated, and misunderstood by others. It's a plea for God to be your protector, vindicator, and righteous judge.

In Luke 18, the Lord tells a story that illustrates David's approach to God in Psalm 28. A poor widow needed a judge to help her obtain justice. The judge, however, was corrupt. He knew she was poor and couldn't afford to bribe him so he refused to hear her case. But she kept pounding on his door, making a nuisance of herself and disturbing his sleep.

Finally, just to silence her, he gave in and gave the woman the justice she sought. He did the right thing—for the wrong reasons.

What was Jesus saying in this parable? He was not suggesting that God is corrupt and unjust. In fact, He knew His listeners would know that God is the exact opposite of this judge. God is just. God is fair. God is compassionate. God always does right by His children. So if an unjust and corrupt judge will do the right thing because of this woman's obstinate insistence, how much *more* will a righteous, holy, compassionate judge do right by us when we cry out to Him for justice?

Jesus told this story to teach us that we must *never* give up in prayer. God, who is just and compassionate, answers persistent prayers for justice. If your prayer is consistent with the *Word* of God, then your prayer will be consistent with the *will* of God. He always keeps His promises.

The Form of David's Prayer

Psalm 28 is a prayer in the form of a song, which can be divided into three sections. Each section deals with a specific theme:

David places his confident request before the Lord (vv. 1–2).

David presents a well-reasoned case before the Lord (vv. 3–5).

David receives cause for rejoicing from the Lord (vv. 6–9).

David's Confident Request

First, let's look at David's confident request in verses 1–2. It's important to see that David's confidence is not based on his own righteousness nor the rightness of his cause. His confidence is based on *Who God is*. "To you, Lord, I call," he writes. "You are my Rock." In the previous chapter we saw Hannah use this same imagery to describe God: "There is no Rock like our God." A rock is a symbol of the changelessness, permanence, immovability, and invincibility of God.

There is an actor, a former wrestling star and football player, who goes by the name of The Rock. He has built quite a career for himself as an action hero, portraying characters of extraordinary strength, stamina, and physical prowess.

I have no doubt that if The Rock and I squared off against each other in a wrestling ring, they would have to carry me out on a stretcher.

But I can tell you this without fear of contradiction: the man who calls himself The Rock is not changeless, not permanent, and not immovable, nor is he invincible. He is a human being. His stage name is sheer hyperbole, designed to make him more marketable to the public. Only God truly deserves to be called a rock in the sense that David and Hannah use the term. Only God is truly an invisible fortress, a stronghold of safety in times of trouble.

David's world was falling apart—but God was his Rock.

David's family was collapsing—but God was his Rock.

David's government was crumbling—but God was his Rock.

David's throne had been stolen from him—but God was his Rock.

David's subjects had turned against him—but God was his Rock.

Do you know how David felt? Have you ever been betrayed by a family member? Have you ever lost your reputation? Have you ever lost your job and your authority? Have people ever turned against you because they believed the lies told about you? Have you ever felt your world was falling apart?

No matter how people may fail you or mistreat you, God is your fortress. His power never diminishes. His love for you never changes. His support for you never wavers. His mercy toward you never fades. He is your Rock.

Here is a question to consider: When your world is falling apart all around you, how do you respond? Do you run to God, or do you blame Him?

When you find yourself facing the consequences of your own wrong choices, do you cry out to the Rock of ages, or do you blame God for not protecting you from the results of your actions? Do you run to the Rock for refuge, or do you kick at the Rock in frustration?

It all comes down to this simple question: Do you know Who God is?

Our culture abounds with false, unbiblical images of God, and many Christians have unconsciously absorbed these falsehoods about Him. Many of these false images of God are rooted in the attitude of entitlement so many people have today.

We live in an entitlement culture, and people today feel they should have everything handed to them on a silver platter. People with an entitlement mentality never achieve anything for themselves. They wait for others to do it all for them. And they have the same sense of entitlement toward God. After all, He owns all the riches in the world, and He has unlimited power. So He owes us a lifetime of wealth, health, and comfort, right? Wrong! God owes us nothing. We owe Him everything. People with an entitlement mentality toward God do not understand Who God is.

But David understood God very well. He prayed, "Hear my cry for mercy as I call to you for help." A cry for mercy is the farthest thing imaginable from the demand, "You owe me." David knew that if God did not hear him, he had no hope. He might as well be dead. I fully identify with David's emotions. Many times I have cried out to God and said, "Without Your mercy and grace, I am a dead man walking." There are so many times when I have failed the Lord so completely that I have gone to Him not just on my knees but prostrate on my face, saying, "Lord, I have no right to ask for anything except Your promise of mercy. The only confidence I have is in Your unearned, unmerited grace. The only assurance I have is in Your unconditional love."

David wrote Psalm 28 at a time when his soul had been stretched thin by waiting. God had been silent for a while. David was asking Him, begging Him to break the silence and answer his prayer. "For if you remain silent," he writes, "I will be like those who go down to the pit." In other words, if David didn't hear an answer from God, if the Lord did not break His silence, David was as good as dead.

He goes on to say, "I call to you for help, as I lift up my hands toward your Most Holy Place." Raising his hands toward God's Holy Place, the symbol of God's presence, is a passionate plea for God's presence and urgent action in his life.

Raising our hands in prayer turns prayer into work. It's not easy to keep our hands raised. We quickly grow tired. Our arms shake. This is the lesson Moses exemplifies in Exodus 17. As Moses stood on the mountain and raised his hands toward heaven, God gave Joshua the victory down on the plains of battle. But when Moses grew tired and lowered his arms, the battle went against Joshua. Moses needed helpers to raise his arms, to strengthen him for the work of prayer, so that Joshua could defeat the enemy on the plains below.

Prayer is hard work, tiring work, physical work—but prayer is essential to victory. David prayed with his arms raised, putting his mind, spirit, and body into his prayer. He was not just saying a prayer; he was *struggling* in prayer.

In Genesis 32 Jacob wrestled with God all night at a place called Peniel. His struggle is a metaphor illustrating how we must sometimes wrestle with God in prayer. Jacob refused to let go of God, and God heard him and gave him a new name, Israel.

Jesus struggled in the Garden of Gethsemane, so that sweat like blood poured off His body. He wrestled with the horrors of becoming sin for the sake of the whole human race. After His struggle, He submitted to the cross. Then three days later He exploded from the tomb in resurrection power.

Hard work, struggle, suffering, wrestling with God—these difficult experiences are often the prerequisites to victory. We desperately need to understand what it means to persist in prayer as David did.

David's Well-Reasoned Case

Next, let's look at the calm and well-reasoned case David lays out before the Lord in verses 3–5. In this section, David talks about the wicked—people who smile on the outside while plotting evil in their hearts. He asks God to judge them and "repay them for their deeds" and "bring back on them what they deserve."

David's words sound harsh in our ears today. Why is that? Because Satan has sold our generation a bill of goods. He has launched a successful propaganda campaign that has corrupted the thinking of an entire generation. In our media, our government, and our schools, our leaders preach a kind of moral insanity. They say, "The only sin is the sin of being judgmental and intolerant. You must never judge anyone for anything. We must never judge the drug abuser for getting hooked on drugs, never criticize the fornicator for his sexual sin, never blame the criminal for his life of crime, and never condemn the terrorist for taking innocent lives. They don't need your judgment; they need your understanding. They are victims of society and can't help what they do."

In contrast, David says, "Repay them for what their hands have done." How barbaric, how unenlightened, how intolerant of David! He shouldn't be so judgmental toward the people who are hunting him down and trying to take his life. He should be more understanding and tolerant toward them.

On May 22, 2017, a radical Muslim terrorist detonated a homemade shrapnel bomb in a crowd of people at the Manchester Arena in England. People were just leaving a concert by an American pop singer, and the crowd was composed largely of teenage music fans. Twenty-two innocent people were killed and more than 250 were injured.

After the attack, teachers in England were encouraged to use a book, *Talking about Terrorism*, to help elementary school children gain a perspective on the attack. The curriculum told the children not to judge the terrorists but to try to understand their motives. Children were told to write a letter to a terrorist (purely as an exercise) and ask six questions to help the child better understand the terrorist and not judge him. The children were also told that the terrorists killed people because they felt they were unfairly treated and not shown respect. The teaching materials were designed to help children respect the terrorists, and the book compared terrorists to South African leader Nelson Mandela and early twentieth-century women who fought for the right to vote.[2]

A culture that refuses to label the killing of innocent people as evil and that teaches its children to be nonjudgmental toward terrorists is lost. Who benefits from a nonjudgmental view of good and evil? Who is constantly trying to persuade the human race to rationalize and justify all sorts of evil? Who has been selling this propaganda since the Garden of Eden? Satan, of course. Anyone who cannot or will not recognize the devil's authorship behind the judge-nothing-and-tolerate-everything movement is deluded.

Rabbi Jeffrey K. Salkin of Temple Solel in Hollywood, Florida, reports with sadness that Jewish youth have largely succumbed to the moral madness of nonjudgmentalism. He writes:

> I have heard Jewish teenagers tell me: "We have no right to judge the Nazis, because they thought that what they were doing was right."
> Post-modernism has triumphed.
> There are no truths. Just opinions. . . .
> Isaiah knew what he was talking about. . . . "Ah, those who call evil good, and good evil; who present darkness as light and light as darkness; who present bitter as sweet and sweet as bitter! Ah, those who are so wise—in their own opinion; so clever—in their own judgment!" [see Isa. 5:20–21].[3]

God's Word, from cover to cover, commands us to call sin by its rightful name. We are to judge the sin in our lives, and we are to confront sin in the lives of others, not out of a sense of self-righteousness and arrogance but in a spirit of abject humility.

Many people quote the words of Jesus in Matthew 7 out of context, frequently in the King James Version: "Judge not, that ye be not judged." But Jesus was not telling us that we should never judge evil. He was teaching us not to be self-righteous hypocrites. He was warning us that the same standard of judgment we apply to other people, God will apply to us. In the Sermon on the Mount, He says:

> Do not judge, or you too will be judged. For in the same way you judge others, you will be judged, and with the measure you use, it will be measured to you.
>
> Why do you look at the speck of sawdust in your brother's eye and pay no attention to the plank in your own eye? (vv. 1–3)

These biblical principles are consistent with the prayer of David in Psalm 28. David reasons with God, and his reasoning does not rest on his own self-righteousness but on the true and absolute righteousness of God. David has already confessed his own sinfulness to God. But he did not begin his prayer by asking God to judge the wicked. Instead, he begins by asking God to keep him from being dragged into the evil schemes of the wicked.

David is aware of the plank in his own eye. David is conscious of his own propensity to sin. He knows he is capable of behaving as sinfully as the wicked do. That's why he begins by confessing that apart from the life-giving and sustaining power of God's Word, God's Spirit, and God's amazing mercy he would be swept away with the wicked.

Please don't miss what David is saying in this prayer. He is praying for justice against the wicked. And he is not praying on behalf of himself as a private citizen, but as the rightful king of Israel. He is God's chosen leader of God's chosen people. As the rightful leader of the nation, King David had a responsibility to execute justice, to defend the oppressed and powerless, and to judge and punish the guilty. As the apostle Paul wrote to the Christians in Rome: "For the one in authority is God's servant for your good. But if you do wrong, be afraid, for rulers do not bear the sword for no reason. They are God's servants, agents of wrath to bring punishment on the wrongdoer" (Rom. 13:4).

It is not God's will that evildoers go unpunished. It is not His will that they prosper. When we pray for the evil plans of wicked people to be frustrated and destroyed, we are praying in perfect alignment with the will of God, as He has stated in His Word.

Many people today, including many who profess to be Christians, demonstrate a misplaced compassion toward criminals that is nothing less than cruelty toward innocent victims. Some of these people want to protect the civil rights of the wicked without regard to the rights of the innocent to be safe and secure in their homes. They care more about rapists than rape victims. They care more about child abusers than children. They care more about cop killers than cops.

Excusing evil is itself an evil act. Pray according to the sound reasoning and wisdom of King David. Pray that God would raise leaders of moral sanity, who feel a righteous indignation toward evil and who act according to biblical principles, not misplaced compassion.

"Hate what is evil; cling to what is good" (Rom. 12:9).

David's Cause for Rejoicing

Finally, let's look at David's cause for rejoicing in the Lord in verses 6–9. When we are in trouble, we cry out to God, and we ask others to intercede for us as well. Then, when He answers our prayer for help, we are thrilled, we rejoice, and we are full of thanksgiving.

But those exuberant emotions fade as time passes. As our gratitude diminishes and our memories grow a bit fuzzy, we can easily fall into a lazy and unfocused prayer life. Oh, we still remember how God delivered us from our trouble, way back when. But what has He done for us lately?

In Luke 17 we find the story of the ten lepers who were healed by Jesus. Only one of the ten—a Samaritan, a foreigner to the covenant people of Israel—came back to say "Thank you" to Jesus. What of the other nine? I don't know why they weren't as grateful as the one. The text doesn't tell us. Perhaps they felt that the world owed them something.

But you won't find that attitude in David's prayer. He begins to praise and thank God even before there is any evidence that his prayers are being answered.

I once prayed for a situation for a considerable length of time. I knew I was praying according to God's will. I knew my prayer was consistent with God's Word. Yet no answer came. I became exasperated. Why wasn't God answering?

Then the Lord laid a thought on my heart: *Why not thank Him now? Why wait until He answers my prayer? He has promised to answer and He always keeps His promises and I believe in His promises. I might as well thank Him now, even though there isn't even a hint of evidence that this prayer will be answered.*

So I prayed my prayer of thanksgiving, expressing heartfelt gratitude to God for an answer to prayer that had not yet arrived. I prayed this prayer of thanksgiving for days . . . then weeks . . . then months.

In fact, I prayed my prayer of thanksgiving for more than eighteen months without any hint, any sign, that my prayer was being answered.

Those were difficult days. The devil taunted me. I could sense him saying to me, *How can you thank God when He is taking forever to answer your prayer? How can you be grateful for months and months of silence from heaven? You're wasting your breath, praying and thanking God. Face it, He isn't listening.*

Yet when my prayer was finally answered, when Satan was again proved to be a liar, I was so glad I had persevered in prayer—and that I had persevered in giving thanks for an answer that lay in the future. I was so grateful to God that He gave me the faith to keep thanking Him through those long months of waiting.

In verses 6–7 of Psalm 28, David expresses the emotions that fill him as he prays:

> Praise be to the LORD,
>   for he has heard my cry for mercy.
> The LORD is my strength and my shield;
>   my heart trusts in him, and he helps me.
> My heart leaps for joy,
>   and with my song I praise him.

David is filled with exuberant praise because the Lord has heard him and helped him in the past. Moreover, David's heart is full of trusting affection for the Lord because He helps David in the present. And David adds that his heart leaps for joy—so much joy that he must express his emotions in a song.

For now, during our sojourn on earth, we live our lives in the time dimension. We are where we are today because of what God did for us yesterday. We will be at a new place tomorrow because of what God is doing for us today. But God is not trapped in the time dimension as we are. He sees the past, the present, and the future at the same time. We can't see what's going to happen in the next minute, much less a year or a decade from now—*but He can*. He sees what we can't see; He knows what we can't know. So we need to trust His will for our lives. We need to keep our hearts bound to God's heart through prayer so that we can know His will for our lives and follow His will confidently and obediently.

And as we pray for God's direction in our own lives, let's not miss the blessing of interceding for others. When we pray for others, when we uphold each other in prayer, we experience a blessing we can never know by any other means on earth. When we pray for God's work, we become partners with God in His plan for history. When we pray for other people, we ask God to move in their lives in a supernatural way, and we show love to them in a way nothing else can match.

When we pray, we take a step away from this planet, with all of its distractions and sorrows and sufferings, and we set foot in the heavenly realm. We approach the throne of grace, and we commune directly, heart to heart, with God the Father. And when we bring the needs of our friends and loved ones and even strangers before His throne and lay them out for Him to see and to touch, we bring these souls close to the loving heart of God.

David concludes his prayer by interceding for others: "Save your people and bless your inheritance; be their shepherd and carry them forever." These are the words of the shepherd-king, who as a boy saved many helpless lambs from the jaws of lions and bears and carried them home in his arms.

Rock of Ages

In 2002, Queen Elizabeth II celebrated her Golden Jubilee, the fiftieth anniversary of her coronation as queen in 1952.

It was a global party celebrated in the British Isles, Australia, New Zealand, Jamaica, Canada, and even outside the British Commonwealth. The televised concert on the grounds of Buckingham Palace celebrated a half century of pop music with rock-and-roll stars, including Paul McCartney, Eric Clapton, and Cliff Richard. There was no mention of the glory of God, and some of the performers engaged in vulgar language and behavior. If Queen Elizabeth saw and heard everything that was sung and done in her "honor," she was probably embarrassed.

Contrast Queen Elizabeth's Golden Jubilee celebration with that of Queen Victoria in 1887. At her celebration, she received kings, princes, and elected leaders from around the world for a worship and commemoration service at Westminster Abbey. She requested a song be sung by the head of the Madagascar delegation. As he began to sing, Queen Victoria wept openly.

What was the song that evoked tears from England's queen? It was a Christian hymn, "Rock of Ages," first sung in 1763.

> Rock of Ages, cleft for me,
> Let me hide myself in Thee;
> Let the water and the blood,
> From Thy riven side which flowed,
> Be of sin the double cure,
> Cleanse me from its guilt and power.

Those words were written by an Anglican cleric named Augustus Toplady. He came to Christ at age sixteen while a student at Trinity College in Dublin, Ireland, after hearing a sermon entitled "The Lord Our Rock." Toplady was frail and chronically afflicted with tuberculosis. He rarely knew a day when he was free from pain. He studied for the ministry, and he had a passion to preach the gospel. But his illness rendered him too weak, too short of breath to stand before a congregation and preach. He died at age thirty-eight, fifteen years after writing his most famous and beloved hymn, "Rock of Ages."

It's the song of a sick and suffering young man who desperately wanted to impact the world for Christ—and through its words, he did. It's the song that made tears flow freely down the face of Queen Victoria. And it's a song that recalls the opening lines of another great song, the song of the shepherd-king, Psalm 28: "To you, LORD, I call; you are my Rock."

The Lord is our Rock, our strength, and our shield! We trust Him and He helps us! Our hearts leap for joy, and with our songs and our prayers, we praise Him!

4

DANIEL

A Prayer of Confession and Repentance

Daniel 9

The courts have, in effect, repealed the First Amendment.
What the Constitution calls "the free exercise" of religion
is now a firing offense in America. That is what high school
football coach Joe Kennedy found out in 2015.

Coach Kennedy taught in the Bremerton School District
of Washington State. After every game, he would go to the
fifty-yard line and take a knee for about thirty seconds. With
his head bowed, he would silently thank God for a good
game and that no players had been injured on either side.
Then he'd get up and be on his way.

He didn't preach. There was no altar call, no choir singing "Just as I Am." There was just a half a minute of silent
prayer by a coach who cared about the well-being of his
players. Yes, there were still fans in the stands. There were

still players on the field. Sometimes, players would join him at midfield and bow their heads alongside him, but that was purely voluntary on their part. Coach Kennedy never invited anyone to join him. No player ever felt pressured to take part.

No one should have been offended by this simple expression of constitutionally protected religious expression. But, of course, Satan is always offended when God's people pray. And he is always looking for ways to outlaw even the silent prayers of Christians.

In 2015, after years of praying at midfield after games without any complaints, Coach Kennedy was confronted by district officials and told he must stop exercising his faith on the football field. If he wanted to wait until all the players were off the field and all the fans had emptied the bleachers, then he could pray for as long as he wanted at the fifty-yard line. But if he continued these prayers in view of the players and fans, he would be suspended.

I don't think the people who make these rules have ever read the actual wording of the First Amendment. Here is the full text: "Congress shall make no law respecting an establishment of religion, or prohibiting the free exercise thereof; or abridging the freedom of speech, or of the press; or the right of the people peaceably to assemble, and to petition the government for a redress of grievances." These words don't guarantee the *private* exercise of religion. They guarantee the *free* exercise of religion. Free means free. Our freedom of religion cannot be prohibited. If we can't bow our heads and silently pray in public without losing our jobs—including jobs in the government sector—then *we are not free.*

Coach Kennedy continued to pray silently for about thirty seconds at midfield after games. He was not establishing a state-sponsored religion. He wasn't suggesting that the school endorse his religious expression. He was simply exercising his faith and his First Amendment freedom. In response, the school district suspended him. When his contract came up for renewal, the district refused to renew it. Make no mistake: this is nothing less than state-sponsored persecution of religion.

Seeking to be rehired, Coach Kennedy took his case through the courts until it finally reached a three-judge panel of the Ninth Circuit Court of Appeals in San Francisco. The court ruled against him. One judge wrote: "When Kennedy kneeled and prayed on the fifty-yard line immediately after games while in view of students and parents, he spoke as a public employee, not as a private citizen, and his speech therefore was constitutionally unprotected."[1] That is a false rationalization; no one at the games thought that Coach Kennedy's prayers at the fifty-yard line were expressions of school policy or an attempt to establish a school religion. He clearly acted as a private citizen.

The consequences of this decision, if the ruling is applied evenly to all high school coaches of all religions in America, could be far reaching and devastating. A Catholic coach could be fired for crossing himself or wearing a cross or religious medal at a game. A female Muslim coach wearing a headscarf or a male Jewish coach wearing a yarmulke also risks career loss. Because of this decision, all public school coaches across America have essentially lost their First Amendment religious freedom.

It has been said that many sins are not crimes—and many crimes are not sins. It is not a sin to pray, but increasingly it has become a *crime* to pray. I love the slogan I once saw printed on the front of a T-shirt: "If prayer is a crime, then

I'll do the time." On the back of the T-shirt were these words, adapted from 1 Peter 3:13–14: "If you suffer for what is right, you are blessed. Do not fear their threats. Do not be afraid."

This is the lesson of the life of the Old Testament prophet Daniel. He lived in dangerous times. Like Coach Kennedy, Daniel was a public official bound by the rules of the government he served. Like Coach Kennedy, Daniel was told that it was a crime to pray to God. But unlike Coach Kennedy, it wasn't just Daniel's career that was on the line—it was his *life*.

Prayer became a crime in the land of Babylon, and Daniel was ready to sacrifice his life to pray publicly in defiance of the law. Daniel was a righteous lawbreaker. He flagrantly flouted the king's law because that law violated the law of God.

When prayer becomes a crime, God calls you and me to become master criminals. When the godless authorities accuse us of the crime of praying to our God, may we stand boldly before our accusers and righteously answer, "Guilty as charged!"

Making a Righteous Spectacle of Prayer

Some four centuries ago, John Owen, an English theologian, wrote, "What a minister is on his knees in secret before God Almighty, that he is and no more."[2] That's a powerful, convicting statement—but why limit it only to ministers? I would alter the wording slightly: "What *Christians* are on their knees in secret before God Almighty, that they are and no more."

The Old Testament prophet Daniel was a great man of God and a great man of prayer. He became an advisor to kings because of who he was in secret on his knees before God. Daniel was born in the land of Judah, the southern kingdom, during a time when much of the nation had fallen away from God. He was a youth, a teenager, when God permitted the forces of King Nebuchadnezzar of Babylon to sweep into the nation and lay siege to Jerusalem. The Babylonians conquered Jerusalem, destroyed the city walls, and razed the great temple of Solomon.

Along with much of the population of Jerusalem, Daniel and his friends were shackled and led away in chains to Babylon, where they became servants in the royal court of Nebuchadnezzar. Exiled to a foreign land, forced to serve a godless king, immersed in an idolatrous and demon-worshiping culture with unimaginable pressures placed on him to conform to Babylonian ways, Daniel stood firm. He stood his moral and spiritual ground as a teenager, and when he reached old age, he was still standing his moral and spiritual ground. He never faltered, never yielded to the false religions of that land, despite many threats to his life. Whenever you see a person standing firm for God, you'll find that they first bent the knee to God in prayer.

One of the most memorable crises in Daniel's life is recounted in Daniel 6, and it centers on the issue of prayer. By this time, Daniel was no longer a young man. He had lived in Babylon for more than sixty years and had served several kings. By this time, the kingdom of Babylon had been conquered by the Persians under Darius the Mede. Daniel had proven himself so capable, honest, and trustworthy that he had risen to a very high position in the Persian government. The vast Persian Empire was divided into 120 regions or satraps, and the satraps had been apportioned to three overseers. Daniel was one of those three trusted overseers. He was, in many ways, a kind of assistant king.

There were a number of high officials in the Persian government who bitterly resented Daniel. He was an outsider from the defeated nation of Judah, and the king had passed over many qualified native-born Persians to elevate this Hebrew. Daniel's rivals tried to find some fault to accuse him of, but his record was spotless. So they decided to use his faithfulness to God against him.

I once had a conversation with a talented young Christian businessman. After being with his company for more than a dozen years, he realized he had hit an invisible ceiling and was stuck there, unable to advance any higher in the company. Less-qualified people were being promoted ahead of him, and when he asked why, his superiors told him to be patient. Finally, a coworker confided to him that he was deliberately being held back because of his reputation for honesty. His bosses knew that he would never lie or cheat his customers, so he was being denied promotions. "I'll never advance any higher with the company," he told me, "but I have the consolation of knowing I have a Christian testimony and a reputation for integrity."

A reputation for godliness and integrity is not always a career advantage in this fallen world as Daniel discovered. Daniel's rivals maneuvered King Darius into proclaiming a law making it illegal for anyone in the empire to pray to any god or man other than Darius himself. The law would be in effect for thirty days, then people could return to their normal religious practices. The idea of requiring the entire empire to bow and pray to Darius appealed to the Persian king's narcissistic ego. The penalty for breaking the law?

Death in the lions' den. The decree was irreversible under Persian law; once it was proclaimed, even the king himself could not revoke it.

Why did Daniel's enemies make it illegal to pray to God? They knew Daniel's habits and his character. They knew he prayed three times a day—morning, noon, and night. He always prayed facing Jerusalem, the city of his childhood. Daniel remembered Jerusalem as the site of the great temple. He gave thanks to God and asked God for help. Whenever a believer takes the time, three times a day, to thank God and ask Him for help, you know that this person is a serious follower of the Lord. This is a believer who talks to God—and listens for His answers.

When Daniel heard that King Darius had outlawed prayer to God, the first thing he did was to defy the law boldly and publicly. As was his habit, he went upstairs in his house, opened the shutters of his window, and proceeded to pray. His rivals came and found Daniel praying and perhaps took notes on everything he said. They wanted to be sure they had Daniel dead to rights.

Then they hurried to the palace and reported everything they had seen and heard to Darius himself. The king was grief-stricken. Daniel was his most trusted advisor and administrator. When proclaiming that law, Darius had never considered that Daniel would be snared by it and have to die.

Daniel's Amazing Consistency

Daniel easily could have rationalized a compromise solution to this dilemma. He could have said to himself, *This law is only in effect for thirty days. God will understand if I take a month off from thanking Him and asking Him for help. He wouldn't expect me to keep praying to Him if it meant I'd end up as lion chow. I'll just resume my daily devotions next month.*

Or he might have thought, *I'll just keep my devotional life quiet for a month. I'll shut the window, hide in the closet, and pray silently. That way, God will still hear me. Sure, it's a little cowardly, but I'll just confess my cowardice and repent of it thirty days from now.*

Isn't that how many of us, as Christians, rationalize our moral compromises today? But Daniel refused to compromise. In fact, he made a spectacle of himself. No one could have any doubt that Daniel was breaking the law and praying to God. Daniel refused to pray to any human being, including the king of Persia. He would never obey a human law that violated the law of God. He became a righteous lawbreaker, a master criminal in the service of his God.

Daniel was amazingly consistent throughout his life. That's what his enemies were counting on. He consistently honored God. He consistently prayed three times a day. He consistently offered praise. He consistently prayed for God's help. He consistently witnessed to the world about the glory and majesty and supremacy of his God. And he consistently refused to compromise his principles and beliefs.

It was the integrity and consistency of Daniel's prayer life that made him such a wise and dependable servant to King Darius—and that made him such a threat to his rivals. Daniel's enemies counted on his integrity in order to trap him. It broke King Darius's heart to have to carry out the punishment of the decree. It also must have angered him to realize he had been maneuvered into sacrificing his finest servant on the altar of his own foolish ego. He walked with Daniel to the mouth of the lions' den and said to him before the guards threw him to the beasts, "May your God, whom you serve continually, rescue you!" (Dan. 6:16).

Then Daniel was thrown in, and the lions' den was covered with a heavy stone sealed with the king's own signet ring. That night, the king could neither eat nor sleep. At dawn, the king hurried to the lions' den. He had the stone removed, and then he called out to Daniel.

And Daniel answered! "May the king live forever!" he said. "My God sent his angel, and he shut the mouths of the lions. They have not hurt me, because I was found innocent in his sight" (vv. 21–22).

So Daniel was lifted from the den, alive and well, and the king had Daniel's rivals brought to the lions' den to take his place. So the lions dined on Persian food instead of kosher food that day. King Darius then wrote a new proclamation and had it issued in every known language on earth:

I issue a decree that in every part of my kingdom people must fear and reverence the God of Daniel.

For he is the living God
   and he endures forever;
his kingdom will not be destroyed,
   his dominion will never end.
He rescues and he saves;
   he performs signs and wonders
   in the heavens and on the earth.
He has rescued Daniel
   from the power of the lions. (vv. 26–27)

When God's people refuse to compromise their faith, when God's people obey the laws of God over the laws of man, when God's people persistently, consistently, and obstinately go to their knees in prayer, *big things happen*. Future history changes.

Daniel could not have been certain that God would spare him from the jaws of the hungry lions. I believe he went into that den of lions with a mindset of resignation, thinking he was almost certainly going to die. Yes, he had seen God miraculously rescue three of his friends from a fiery furnace (Dan. 3). But even they had gone into the furnace saying that, whether God rescued them or not, even if they died in the flames, they would never worship a false god.

It's interesting to note that there is a prayer offered for Daniel's rescue from the lions—but Daniel does not pray that prayer. Who does? Darius himself! He says to Daniel, "May your God, whom you serve continually, rescue you!" Though the words are directed at Daniel, the plea is directed toward God. Darius, who has forbidden prayers to any god other than himself, now offers an invocation to Daniel's God. The king has broken his own law as surely as Daniel has.

Prayers That Will Be Heard—and Answered

The theme of this book is the life-changing prayers of ordinary people in the Bible. Now, you may look at Daniel and say, "There's nothing ordinary about this man. He's one of the most extraordinary people in history—extraordinary in his faith, extraordinary in his fearlessness, extraordinary in his fidelity to God."

I fully understand that point of view, yet I believe Daniel was truly an ordinary human being. Yes, his accomplishments were extraordinary, but that's because Daniel was an ordinary man with an extraordinary commitment to prayer. He refused to compromise his thrice-daily conversations with God. He wouldn't let anything or anyone—not even the king of Persia—come between him and his God.

Aside from his extraordinary commitment to prayer, Daniel was no different from you and me. Everything else that was notable about Daniel flowed from his daily time with God. People who spend time with God every day can't help but be changed.

Daniel was essentially a bureaucrat, a government functionary. He was not so much a leader as a manager. The king was the leader—whether that king was Nebuchadnezzar, Belshazzar, Darius, or Cyrus. Daniel's job was to see that the directives of the king were faithfully executed. He was skilled at his work, but not extraordinarily so. He had talents and abilities, but so did many of his Persian coworkers.

I believe it was his intense commitment to prayer that made him stand out. The time he spent alone with God polished his character so that his integrity was as brilliant and unbreakable as a diamond. The time he spent alone with God deepened his wisdom and insight into matters of governing, diplomacy, and statecraft. The time he spent alone with God strengthened his courage and boldness so that he feared no man, not even the king. And as we're about to see, the time he spent alone with God gave him a special understanding of God's Word and God's will.

God achieved extraordinary things through Daniel for one reason and one reason only: *Daniel prayed*. After Daniel prayed, God gave him the ability to interpret dreams. After Daniel prayed, God sealed shut the jaws of hungry lions and opened the king's eyes to the power and majesty of Daniel's God. And we're about to see that, after Daniel prayed, God revealed to him the outline of future history, including the precise date that Jesus would enter Jerusalem as king of the Jews. Daniel was an ordinary man, but his consistent prayer life transformed him into an extraordinary prophet.

Turning to Daniel 9, we find Daniel once again caught in the act of prayer. Daniel tells us that it is the first year of the reign of King Darius over the Babylonian kingdom. Daniel has been studying the scroll of Jeremiah the prophet, and he makes an amazing discovery. Jeremiah, under the inspiration of the Holy Spirit, prophesies that the desolation of Jerusalem, which began when Nebuchadnezzar laid siege to the city, will last seventy years. How long have the Jewish people been exiled in Babylon? Nearly seventy years.

So Daniel puts on sackcloth and ashes, forgoes his meals, and fasts for several days. During this time, he pleads with God in prayer. This is Daniel's heartfelt prayer:

> LORD, the great and awesome God, who keeps his covenant of love with those who love him and keep his commandments, we have sinned and done wrong. We have been wicked and have rebelled; we have turned away from your commands and laws. We have not listened to your servants the prophets, who spoke in your name to our kings, our princes and our ancestors, and to all the people of the land.
>
> LORD, you are righteous, but this day we are covered with shame—the people of Judah and the inhabitants of Jerusalem and all Israel, both near and far, in all the countries where you have scattered us because of our unfaithfulness to you.

We and our kings, our princes and our ancestors are covered with shame, LORD, because we have sinned against you. The LORD our God is merciful and forgiving, even though we have rebelled against him; we have not obeyed the LORD our God or kept the laws he gave us through his servants the prophets. All Israel has transgressed your law and turned away, refusing to obey you.

Therefore the curses and sworn judgments written in the Law of Moses, the servant of God, have been poured out on us, because we have sinned against you. You have fulfilled the words spoken against us and against our rulers by bringing on us great disaster. Under the whole heaven nothing has ever been done like what has been done to Jerusalem. Just as it is written in the Law of Moses, all this disaster has come on us, yet we have not sought the favor of the LORD our God by turning from our sins and giving attention to your truth. The LORD did not hesitate to bring the disaster on us, for the LORD our God is righteous in everything he does; yet we have not obeyed him.

Now, LORD our God, who brought your people out of Egypt with a mighty hand and who made for yourself a name that endures to this day, we have sinned, we have done wrong. LORD, in keeping with all your righteous acts, turn away your anger and your wrath from Jerusalem, your city, your holy hill. Our sins and the iniquities of our ancestors have made Jerusalem and your people an object of scorn to all those around us.

Now, our God, hear the prayers and petitions of your servant. For your sake, LORD, look with favor on your desolate sanctuary. Give ear, our God, and hear; open your eyes and see the desolation of the city that bears your Name. We do not make requests of you because we are righteous, but because of your great mercy. LORD, listen! LORD, forgive! LORD, hear and act! For your sake, my God, do not delay, because your city and your people bear your Name. (Dan. 9:4–19)

Daniel opens his prayer with a confession of sin—the sin of all his people, present and past. He confesses the sins of previous generations, the sins of ancestors, the sins of kings and princes. And he fully identifies with his people. He doesn't say, "*They* have been wicked." He says, "*We* have been wicked" (v. 5, emphasis added).

Daniel prays a prayer of deep humility. He says, "LORD, you are righteous, but this day we are covered with shame" (v. 7). It is a prayer rooted in the truth of Scripture: "The curses and sworn judgments written in the Law of Moses, the servant of God, have been poured out on us, because we have sinned against you" (v. 11).

It is a prayer that acknowledges the power, goodness, and mercy of God toward Israel in the past: "Now, LORD our God, who brought your people out of Egypt with a mighty hand and who made for yourself a name that endures to this day . . . turn away your anger and your wrath" (vv. 15–16).

It is a prayer of abject pleading: "Now, our God, hear the prayers and petitions of your servant" (v. 17).

It is a prayer that begs God to forgive so that His Name would be glorified: "LORD, listen! LORD, forgive! LORD, hear and act! For your sake, my God, do not delay, because your city and your people bear your Name" (v. 19).

In this prayer, Daniel sets a pattern for prayer—confession, intercession, and petition—that the apostle James will prescribe centuries later in his New Testament epistle: "Therefore confess your sins to each other and pray for each other so that you may be healed. The prayer of a righteous person is powerful and effective" (James 5:16). When a Christian believes God, when a Christian trusts and obeys God's Word, that Christian can pray with confidence and power, knowing that those prayers will be heard and answered.

Praying the Promises of God

Once during a community-wide prayer campaign, I gave dozens of radio interviews. I spoke with radio hosts on both religious and secular stations. One of the secular radio hosts asked me an odd question during our interview. I had been talking about the need for Christians to step up and pray, and he said, "You must be looking for some good ones, aren't you?"

I was sure I knew what he meant, but I wasn't sure that the listeners would understand so I said, "Some good ones? What do you mean? Some good what?"

He said, "Some good pray-ers. People who will follow through on their commitment to pray."

"Oh yes," I said. "I'm praying for a lot of good pray-ers, righteous pray-ers. The prayers of the righteous are effective."

When we pray, we must pray with the conviction and confidence of Daniel. We must pray with the expectation that we will see results in prayer. There's no point in doubting the Word of God or the promises of God. (And if you do have doubts, then start with the prayer of the desperate father in Mark 9:24: "I do believe; help me overcome my unbelief!")

Daniel prayed this prayer because he had discovered the scroll of the prophet Jeremiah and had begun reading the prophecy contained therein: "This is what the LORD says:

'When seventy years are completed for Babylon, I will come to you and fulfill my good promise to bring you back to this place'" (Jer. 29:10). Before the fall of Jerusalem, when Jeremiah was warning the people of Judah of God's approaching judgment, they laughed at him, mocked him, persecuted him, and hated him. Some even tried to kill him.

But Daniel read the words of Jeremiah and he believed. Daniel knew that God would keep His word no matter who believed Him, no matter how many people doubted Him, and no matter how many years had passed. Daniel knew that God was faithful, even if God's people were not. Daniel knew that God's Word is true, even if no one believed it.

It's important to catch the irony in Daniel's prayer. When he prayed this prayer of faith, he was one of very few people who believed that God would fulfill His promises. And there were not too many Jews in Babylon who were eager to return to Jerusalem. Though they had come to Babylon in chains, many of them had prospered over the years. Many had become influential and wealthy citizens, first of Babylon and later of the Persian Empire. Some were sunk chin-deep in materialism. They were living the Babylonian lifestyle, and many didn't want to go home.

Ah, but the prayer of a righteous man can accomplish much.

As we examine this prayer of Daniel and use it as a prescription for revitalizing our own experience with prayer, four insights become clear, each beginning with the letter A. Daniel's prayer was anchored in God's promises, affirming of God's glory, assenting to God's mercy, and appealing to God on behalf of others. Let's look at each of these features of Daniel's prayer.

Anchored in God's Promises

Effective prayer—the prayer that God delights in answering—must be firmly anchored in the promises of God. Prayers that violate the letter and spirit of God's promises are nothing but a waste of breath. Daniel's prayer is rooted firmly in the promises of God, which He established in His covenant.

Every great prayer in the Bible makes reference to the covenants God established in the Old Testament. The prayer of Daniel is no exception. For example, in Daniel 9:4 he says, "Lord, the great and awesome God, who keeps his covenant of love with those who love him and keep his commandments." What is God's "covenant of love" that Daniel refers to?

God made several covenants with human beings in the Bible. In Genesis 9, after the flood of Noah, God made a covenant with the entire human race never to destroy the world by flood again, and He placed a rainbow in the sky as a sign of that covenant. In Genesis 12 and 15, God made a covenant with Abraham, granting him the land of promise and promising him a multitude of descendants—a covenant that God would make of Abraham a great nation. In Genesis 17, God gave Abraham the covenant of circumcision, a sign in the flesh of God's everlasting covenant with Abraham. In Numbers 18, we find God's covenant establishing the priesthood of Aaron. And in 2 Samuel 7, God made a covenant establishing David and his descendants as the rightful lineage of the kings of Israel—a lineage that would one day produce the long-awaited Messiah.

But the covenant Daniel refers to, the covenant of love, is God's covenant with Moses in Exodus 19 through 24 and in the book of Deuteronomy. In that covenant, God promised,

"If you obey me fully and keep my covenant, then out of all nations you will be my treasured possession" (Exod. 19:5). As a part of this conditional covenant, known as the Mosaic covenant or the covenant of Moses, God gave the Ten Commandments to Israel, and He gave the Sabbath as an enduring sign of His covenant of love.

A promise is a statement about something that will happen in the future. But the best way to remember God's promises is to recount what has happened in the past. That is what Daniel does. He says, "The LORD our God is merciful and forgiving, even though we have rebelled against him" (Dan. 9:9) and "[You] brought your people out of Egypt with a mighty hand" (v. 15). Daniel recounts God's faithfulness to His promises in the past. He recounts God's salvation of His people in the past. He recounts God's intervention in times of crisis in the past. He recounts God's grace and mercy in forgiving Israel's sins in the past.

Remembering how God has kept His promises in the past makes our prayers effective in the present as we look toward the future. This is especially true regarding God's promise to forgive sin. Again and again throughout this prayer, Daniel confesses the sin of his people. He does not cover it up, explain it away, minimize it, rationalize it, or dismiss it. He abjectly, unreservedly confesses the sin of his people: "We have been wicked and have rebelled; we have turned away from your commands and laws" (v. 5).

Notice that word *wicked*. That's a word we rarely hear anymore. It's certainly a word we would never apply to ourselves. After all, we are good people! We go to church. We put money in the offering plate. We are not mean to anyone, we don't oppress anyone, we don't hurt anyone. In fact, we

are such good people that God is fortunate to have us on
His team!

But Daniel refuses to sugarcoat sinfulness. He will not
pull any punches. *Wickedness* is the right word for the sinfulness of the people. When God judged the people and sent
them into captivity in Babylon, He judged them for their
wickedness.

But Daniel's confession is anchored in the promises of
God. The Lord has promised mercy and forgiveness when
we repent and turn back to Him. As King David wrote after
confessing his sins of adultery and murder to God: "My
sacrifice, O God, is a broken spirit; a broken and contrite
heart you, God, will not despise" (Ps. 51:17). And in the
New Testament, John assures, "If we confess our sins, he is
faithful and just and will forgive us our sins and purify us
from all unrighteousness" (1 John 1:9).

God loves it when His children remind Him of His promises. Why? Is it because God is forgetful? Does He need us
to help Him remember what He promised us? No, there is
no problem with God's memory. But there's a big problem
with ours. We easily forget His promises, and that's when
we fall into the trap of blaming God for our failings.

Many of God's promises are conditional. We often fail to
keep our side of the bargain, then we blame God when He
doesn't give us what we think He has promised us. It's like
blaming the power company for shutting off the electricity
after we stopped paying the bill. "But they promised to keep
the power on! My food is spoiling in the refrigerator! I can't
watch my game shows on TV! I can't charge my phone! And
it's the power company's fault!" No, it's not. If you didn't
keep your end of the covenant and pay the bill, the power

company has no responsibility to honor its promise to supply electricity. The covenant is broken, and *you* broke it.

When we remind God in prayer of His promises, we also remind ourselves of the conditions under which God made those promises and of our responsibility to hold up our end of the covenant. The terms of the covenant make it clear that we cannot excuse ourselves and blame God. Nor can we blame our spouses or the boss or the economy or the weather or any other convenient scapegoat. We have to take personal responsibility for meeting the conditions of God's promises.

When we pray, God wants to hear a confession of our sin. Our confession is always rooted in an awareness of God's promises to forgive, redeem, and restore. Our prayers must be anchored in the promises of God.

Affirming of God's Glory

For many if not most Christians, prayer is either a cry for help or a wish list. Either we are in desperate trouble and we are sending an SOS to heaven, or we are asking God for something we really, really, *really* want. The *last* thing on our minds is the issue that should be *uppermost* in our minds: the glory of God. A spiritually mature and effective prayer life begins with a recognition of God's grandeur, majesty, omniscience, omnipotence, and omnipresence—in short, His glory.

One of the great privileges I have as a minister of the gospel is the joy of praying with and for other people. The pastor of the church has an X-ray view of his congregation because so many of them come to him for counseling and prayer. The pastor becomes aware of the depth of suffering that many of his parishioners endure on a daily basis.

In my humanness, I want to alleviate all the suffering I see. But in my spirit, as I seek to be sensitive to God's Holy Spirit, I pray that God would be glorified, first and foremost. And often, God is glorified through our weakness and our sufferings. When we get to know God as deeply as Daniel knew Him, when we begin to love God as truly as Daniel loved Him, then we begin to care more about God's glory than our own needs and wants. Our prayer life changes. We begin to pray, first and foremost, that God would be glorified through our lives.

God wants His name to be glorified even more than we do. So when we seek first the glory of God, we are aligning *our* wills with *His* will. We are aligning *our* purposes with *His* purpose. We are aligning *our* hearts with *His* heart. We are aligning *our* desires with *His* desires. And that's when God delights in answering our prayers.

Daniel prays, "Now, our God, hear the prayers and petitions of your servant. *For your sake*, Lord, look with favor on your desolate sanctuary" (Dan. 9:17, emphasis added). The phrase I have italicized, *For your sake*, means "For the sake of Your glory." When you hear the phrase *the glory of God*, what do you think of? I find that when most Christians hear these words, they have a vague idea of clouds or a throne or a crown surrounded by radiant light. The phrase seems to have very little content or meaning for many Christians today.

But *the glory of God* is not an empty or vague phrase in the Bible. It is not just God's reputation or His fame. It speaks of God's essential nature and attributes. Bound up in the words *the glory of God* are such concepts as God's sovereignty, omnipotence, omniscience, goodness, justice, beauty, wisdom, and creativity. When we speak of glorifying God, we are saying that we want the whole universe to acknowledge Who God is and what He is like. We glorify God not only by witnessing about Him to our fellow human beings but also by glorifying Him with our lives in front of the invisible rulers and authorities of the spiritual realm—both God's angels and Satan's fallen angels. The apostle Paul writes:

> His intent was that now, through the church, the manifold wisdom of God should be made known to the rulers and authorities in the heavenly realms, according to his eternal purpose that he accomplished in Christ Jesus our Lord. (Eph. 3:10–11)

One of the central purposes for our existence is to glorify God. That is, we are to demonstrate God's true glory, God's true attributes, and God's wisdom and justice before the world and before the rulers and authorities of the spiritual realm. Daniel's desire expressed in this prayer is not a desire for his own wealth, health, or success. There is nothing wrong with wanting to be prosperous, healthy, and successful, but those are not Daniel's chief priorities. His desire is for God's glory.

Daniel goes on to say, "LORD, listen! LORD, forgive! LORD, hear and act! For your sake, my God, do not delay, because your city and your people bear your Name" (Dan. 9:19). Daniel pleads with God to save His people—not because they are deserving, not because they are entitled, and not because they are to be pitied. He pleads with God to save His people for the sake of His own name and His own glory.

In recent years, my daily prayers to God have been intensified with pleas that God would bring glory and honor to Himself. My longing is more and more for His glory. My purpose for living is, more than anything else, to see God glorified and honored.

And as I have prayed, first and foremost, that God would be glorified, I have experienced more effectiveness in my intercession and more answers to my prayers.

Assenting to God's Mercy

Some Christians mistakenly think that when they pray, they need to remind God of all the things they have done for Him. They like to remind God of how useful and faithful they have been to Him and how God really couldn't get along without them. There is not a hint of this attitude in Daniel's prayer.

Daniel's only plea in this prayer is a plea for God's mercy. He knows that his righteousness and the righteousness of his people are as filthy rags. God owes them nothing; they owe God everything. Every blessing they receive comes from the hand of God by the mercy of God.

At the time Daniel prayed this prayer, about sixty-eight years had passed since the beginning of the Babylonian captivity. The Jewish people had been ruled by first the Babylonians, then the Persians. The younger generation of Jews had known only life in Babylon. They knew of the land of Israel and the city of Jerusalem only from the stories their elders told. They were accustomed to the Babylonian lifestyle, the Babylonian culture, and Babylonian foods. This younger generation liked living in Babylon and didn't want to leave.

In many ways, the America we live in today is much like Babylon.

We need a new movement of the Holy Spirit among us. We need a spiritual awakening. We need to remind ourselves and our children and grandchildren about God's past mercies, spiritual awakenings, and interventions.

Daniel prays, "We do not make requests of you because we are righteous, but because of your great mercy" (v. 18). We desperately need to assent to the mercy of God. Mercy is one of His most distinctive covenant characteristics. God loves it when we acknowledge His mercy, ask Him for His mercy, thank Him for His mercy, and assent to His mercy.

A friend told me that he had begun reading through the Bible, starting in Genesis. As he read, he was impressed by how many times the people of Israel failed, and how many times God forgave them, restored them, and showed mercy to them. And you can probably make the same observation about your own life: you have failed Him repeatedly, and He has shown you mercy and forgiveness every time. That has certainly been the story of my walk with Christ.

I could tell you story after story and recount failure after failure, and each would be a testament to the mercy of God in my life.

Appealing to God on Behalf of Others

Even a casual reading of Scripture reveals that in ancient Israel God's people were oblivious to their own desperate need. They were oblivious to the moral peril they put themselves in. Daniel was deeply troubled over the spiritual blindness and obliviousness of his people.

Before we either condemn or pity the people of Daniel's time for their spiritual blindness, we should ask ourselves: Am I just as oblivious as they were? Have I placed myself in spiritual danger without even realizing it?

Most of us today, including most Christians, don't spend much time thinking about our moral and spiritual state. We are too busy thinking about the bad economy, the political bickering in Washington, the worsening race relations and fraying social fabric, the threat of terrorism, and so on. We worry about paying our bills, keeping our jobs, maintaining the car, and other practical concerns. We worry about our health and getting a bad diagnosis from the doctor. We worry about not having enough money saved for retirement.

But how much time do we spend thinking about matters of eternal importance? How much time do we spend in God's Word? How much time do we spend talking to God, glorifying Him, seeking His wisdom, and pursuing His will? All the other things we worry about are temporary, but the things of God are eternal.

Jesus warned against allowing the cares of this world to choke the gospel out of our hearts. We who are spiritually minded and who are focused on the things of God need to be on our knees once a day, twice a day, even three times a day, praying for not only ourselves but also our spouses, our children, our parents and siblings, our extended family members, our brothers and sisters in the church, our neighbors, our coworkers and bosses and employees, and everyone else within our sphere of influence. We need to intercede for them—urgently, desperately, passionately.

Like Daniel's people, the loved ones we pray for may not be aware of their need for God. They may not realize how far they have fallen away from a relationship with Him. They may be oblivious to their spiritual danger. Don't take for granted that they are walking with God. Pray for them. Ask God to open their eyes and give them a spiritual reawakening.

God was gracious to Daniel; He answered Daniel's prayer. Just as the prophet Jeremiah had said, about two years after Daniel prayed this prayer the people of Israel began returning to their homeland. The prayer of a righteous person is powerful and effective—and God answered the prayer of Daniel.

But that's not the end of the story.

After Daniel had fasted and prayed, begging God to return His people to their homeland, the angel Gabriel appeared before Daniel, saying, "Daniel, I have now come to give you insight and understanding. As soon as you began to pray, a word went out, which I have come to tell you, for you are highly esteemed" (Dan. 9:22–23).

Gabriel proceeded to lay out a vision of the future of Israel—and the future of the world. This is the famous vision of the seventy "sevens" or the seventy "weeks" of Daniel's prophecy:

> From the time the word goes out to restore and rebuild Jerusalem until the Anointed One, the ruler, comes, there will be seven "sevens," and sixty-two "sevens." It will be rebuilt with streets and a trench, but in times of trouble. After the sixty-two "sevens," the Anointed One will be put to death and will have nothing. (vv. 25–26)

At first glance, this is a difficult prophecy to understand. But once you understand it, it becomes clear that this is an amazingly precise prophecy of the coming of Jesus the Messiah. No one was able to decipher its meaning until the

1890s, when Scotland Yard assistant police commissioner Sir Robert Anderson published his findings in a book called *The Coming Prince*. To make a long story short, he realized that this prophecy was a countdown to a specific event in history: the coming of the Messiah. The order to "restore and rebuild Jerusalem" referred to a decree issued by King Artaxerxes I of Persia on March 14, 445 BC. The prophecy specified a specific number of years until "the Anointed One," the Messiah, would officially be presented as Israel's King. Anderson calculated that this would take place on Sunday, April 6, AD 32. This date is believed to be Palm Sunday, the day Jesus of Nazareth entered the city of Jerusalem and was hailed by the people as the King of the Jews.

So when God answered Daniel's prayer, He not only opened the door to return the Jewish people to their homeland but also entrusted an incredibly specific outline of future history to Daniel. And Daniel recorded that prophecy here in Daniel 9. Every detail of the prophecy Gabriel told Daniel has been fulfilled with mathematical precision, except for those parts that are yet to be fulfilled in our own future.

When you pray, remember Daniel's prayer. Remember that the same God who answered Daniel's prayers has promised to answer your prayers. Remember that the same God who foretold the outline of future history to Jeremiah and Daniel is in control of your future as well. You can trust Him with your future because He is the One who announced the return of His people to Israel after seventy years of exile, then moved the king of Persia to send them home—precisely on schedule. And He is the One who announced the coming of the Messiah, then sent Him into Jerusalem on Palm Sunday—precisely on schedule.

History never catches God by surprise. When we pray, we become partners in the fulfillment of His eternal plan. So pray like Daniel, rely on God's promises, and expect great things to happen.

And prepare to be amazed.

5

JONAH

A Prayer from the Depths of Despair

Jonah 1:17–2:10

Near the end of Walt Disney's 1940 animated classic *Pinocchio*, there's a scene in which the talking puppet Pinocchio goes searching in the ocean depths for his father, Geppetto the woodcarver. Geppetto has been swallowed by Monstro the whale, and Pinocchio bravely seeks to rescue him.

When we first see Geppetto in the belly of the whale, it is a charming scene. Geppetto is on a flatboat floating on a lake of water in the whale's innards, surrounded by the whale's backbone and rib cage. On his little boat, Geppetto has all the comforts of home—a wood stove to keep him warm, a wooden writing desk, a soft bed, a clothesline on which to hang his damp pants and shirt, and a quill pen and paper with which to write a letter to Pinocchio.

This quaint little scene, beautifully rendered by Mr. Disney's artists, would give you the impression that being shut up in the belly of a whale would not be so bad. True, Geppetto wasn't free to leave his watery prison, but as prisons go, Monstro's belly was not so uncomfortable.

I'm not criticizing Mr. Disney's film; it's a beautiful work of fantasy. But I do think that the idealized image of Geppetto in the belly of the whale might make us forget the horror and terror experienced by the Old Testament prophet Jonah when he was trapped for three days in the belly of a fish. To understand the prayer Jonah prayed from the belly of the fish, we need to understand what he was going through. Once we see clearly the horrific circumstances in which Jonah found himself, we can better appreciate his desperate prayer during his ordeal.

The book of Jonah is undoubtedly the most famous "fish story" in the history of literature. Skeptics and atheists would have us believe it is a fairy tale, just one of many fantastic stories in the Bible that should be taken with a grain of salt. Even some who profess to be Christians claim that the story of Jonah is merely a fable with a nice moral, much like the fables of Aesop.

It seems to me, however, that if you cannot or will not believe that the prophet Jonah was swallowed by a great fish and then vomited up on the land, how do you mentally process an even more astounding claim—the death and resurrection of Jesus Christ? And if you don't believe in the death and resurrection of Jesus Christ, how can you call yourself a Christian? A genuine Christian does not find the miracles of the Bible hard to swallow, any more than the great fish found Jonah hard to swallow.

In the book of Jonah, we meet an ordinary man from Bible times, a plain old Joe named Jonah. He was hardly a hero of the Bible. He was, in fact, more of an antihero. When God told him to go to Nineveh, he ran the other way. Have you ever defied God? Have you ever run away from Him or said to Him, "Leave me alone; I want to go my own way"? If so, you're going to enjoy getting to know Jonah a little better, and you'll appreciate the prayer he prayed from the depths of the sea.

Jonah was not only disobedient and self-willed but also filled with bitterness and resentment. Nineveh was the capital of Assyria, and the Assyrians were deadly enemies of the Israelites. It was the Assyrians who later took the Jews of the northern kingdom of Israel into captivity, about a century before Babylon conquered and exiled the Jews of the southern kingdom of Judah. When God told Jonah to go to Nineveh, it would be as if He said to you today, "Go to the stronghold of the terrorists and preach to them about Jesus." Jonah hated the people of Nineveh, and the last thing he wanted was to save them from the coming judgment.

Jonah rejected God's command, turned his back on Nineveh, and headed in the other direction as fast as he could go. Reaching the coast city of Jaffa (or Joppa), Jonah boarded a ship bound for Tarshish. He did not reach his destination. Instead, he ended up in the last place he ever thought he would be: the belly of a great fish.

Was there ever a more reluctant and disobedient prophet in the Bible than Jonah? You may identify with Jonah. You may think, *Jonah and I have a lot in common. I've made such a mess of God's will for my life. When God tells me go, I stop; when He tells me stop, I go like sixty.* That was

Jonah—disobedient and selfish. When the Ninevites repented and God spared them from His judgment, Jonah got mad and sulked.

But Jonah had one thing going for him. When he was in the belly of the fish, he prayed a powerful and sincere prayer. He had a talk with God that is worthy of our study. God used Jonah in spite of himself because when the crisis was upon him and he had nowhere else to turn, Jonah got serious with God and prayed for all he was worth.

Beyond Explanation

I received Christ as my Lord and Savior in 1964, and I was immediately on fire for the Lord. I would go anyplace and tell anyone, even strangers, what Jesus had done for me.

About two years after my conversion experience, I sensed that God was calling me into full-time Christian ministry—but I didn't want that! I had plans, I had goals, and they didn't include becoming a preacher or a missionary. So, like Jonah, I decided to run from the Lord. I abandoned my faith, stopped witnessing, refused to attend church, rejected fellowship with other believers, stopped praying, and ran from God as fast as I could. This period of rebellion lasted about a year and a half.

I'm so grateful that God, in His tender mercy and grace, would not let me go. He let me wander from Him for about eighteen months, then through the circumstances of my life, He began drawing me back into His loving embrace. Since then, He has led me on an exciting, thrilling adventure of faith beyond anything I could have imagined in my youth.

Today, I look back on the foolish young man I was and think, *What was I thinking? Why did I imagine I could escape from God? What if I had remained in a state of rebellion for the rest of my life? Look at all the blessings of knowing and serving Christ I would have missed.*

To think I actually *feared* God's will for my life! Yet that experience has helped me understand the kind of man Jonah was. I can't judge Jonah too harshly because I have been in Jonah's sandals, and I know exactly how it feels to run away from God.

Jonah was a prophet in Israel during the reign of King Jeroboam II. In 2 Kings 14, we learn that Jonah was called a servant of the God of Israel, and he is identified as "Jonah son of Amittai, the prophet from Gath Hepher" (v. 25), a town just north of Nazareth. God had spoken through Jonah, proclaiming that King Jeroboam II would lead the nation in extending Israel's borders from Lebo Hamath (a village that is now in northeastern Lebanon) to the Dead Sea. So Jonah was a certified, authentic prophet of God, and God had spoken through Jonah in the past.

But when God commanded Jonah to go to Nineveh and prophesy against that city because of the wickedness of its people, Jonah refused. He took off for the coast, thinking he could somehow flee from the presence of the Lord. He booked passage on a ship bound for Tarshish. While the ship was at sea, a storm arose, and Jonah discovered that he could run but he couldn't hide from the Lord. The sailors tried to lighten the ship by dumping their cargo, but they soon suspected that this was no ordinary storm. They cast lots and determined that the reason for their distress was Jonah.

After the lots pointed to him, Jonah admitted that he was to blame for the storm. God was chastening him for his disobedience and his attempt to flee from God. "Pick me up and throw me into the sea," Jonah said, "and it will become calm. I know that it is my fault that this great storm has come upon you" (Jon. 1:12).

The sailors didn't want to drown their passenger. They first tried to row back to shore, but the winds and waves were too fierce. In the end, they prayed to Jonah's God, asking Him not to hold them accountable for Jonah's death, and they tossed him into the sea. Instantly, the sea became calm, and the sailors became more fearful than ever. None of their gods could calm the sea as Jonah's God had done.

What happened next is often interpreted as God's punishment inflicted on Jonah. The wayward prophet sank into the sea and was swallowed by a great fish. Yes, being swallowed by a fish is an unpleasant and punishing experience. But that fish also saved Jonah's life. That fish was a sign of God's love and mercy to Jonah, as well as a sign of God's displeasure with his rebellious choices.

While Jonah was in the belly of the fish, he prayed the prayer we are about to examine. There's nothing that will bring you closer to the Lord than spending time in the belly of a fish—either literally or figuratively.

What was it like for Jonah in the innards of that fish? How could he stay alive for three days inside that creature? The answer is that he couldn't. Even if the fish came to the surface from time to time and gulped air into its stomach (which is incredibly unlikely), there's no way the fish would have maintained enough air supply in its stomach to keep Jonah alive for three days. He certainly would have suffocated.

And the gastric juices in the stomach of the fish would certainly have killed Jonah if suffocation hadn't. Those juices, which contain corrosive hydrochloric acid and pepsin and other digestive enzymes, function the same way as juices in the stomachs of land animals: they break down animal tissues into basic nutrients. Even if Jonah could somehow breathe inside the fish, he would have been slowly digested to death in those juices.

Also, the temperature inside the fish's belly was likely hotter than the maximum safe temperature for a hot tub. The sheer horror of that claustrophobic experience might have been enough to stop the normal human heart. If Jonah had felt like eating anything in that dark, stinking, burning, suffocating environment, he would have had nothing to feast on but sushi and seaweed.

Some people have suggested that Jonah could have survived in the same way a whaler named James Bartley survived a similar experience in the late nineteenth century. The story of Bartley's thirty-six-hour ordeal involves being thrown overboard directly into the jaws of a whale, being swallowed whole, then being cut out of the whale by his shipmates after they had killed the whale and were harvesting its blubber. The story has often been told, including by preachers and Bible teachers, but historical investigators have found numerous holes in the story; it's likely that Bartley made up the tale to get attention.

I have to ask: Why are we looking for historical or scientific rationales to bolster our faith in a miracle of God? Science is incapable of proving a miracle. Jesus Himself attested to the supernatural aspect of Jonah's experience, comparing His own approaching death and miraculous resurrection to Jonah's entombment in the fish:

He answered, "A wicked and adulterous generation asks for a sign! But none will be given it except the sign of the prophet Jonah. For as Jonah was three days and three nights in the belly of a huge fish, so the Son of Man will be three days and three nights in the heart of the earth. The men of Nineveh will stand up at the judgment with this generation and condemn it; for they repented at the preaching of Jonah, and now something greater than Jonah is here." (Matt. 12:39–41)

Some people read the words of Jesus alongside the words of Jonah's prayer, "From deep in the realm of the dead I called for help" (Jon. 2:2), and they conclude that Jonah literally died while he was trapped in the belly of the fish. When he prayed to God for help, he wasn't alive inside the fish, he was in "the realm of the dead" (which the Jews called Sheol). Then God answered Jonah's prayer and caused the fish to vomit Jonah onto the beach, whereupon God resurrected him. This interpretation is plausible, but I tend to think that Jonah was miraculously kept alive in the belly of the fish by God's intervention. The text allows either interpretation.

I don't think we make miracles more credible to skeptics by trying to remove the supernatural dimension and offering a more naturalistic explanation. The miracles of God are beyond explanation. The power of God needs no explanation. It's the power that created the universe, that created the forces of life and death, and that raised Jesus from the dead. God can intervene in those processes in any way He chooses.

If you have been through a storm in your life, if you have found yourself in the belly of the beast, if you are suffering as a consequence of disobedience or even through no fault of your own, then the prayer of Jonah is for you. You'll identify with it, learn from it, and be comforted by it.

That's why I don't want to focus too much on the details of how Jonah survived his ordeal, whether it can be explained in natural terms or whether there are historical precedents for surviving being ingested by a sea creature. If you're going through a time of intense and painful trial right now, none of that matters. But the prayer that Jonah prayed matters a great deal.

So we won't focus so much on what was happening inside the great fish. Instead, we'll focus on what was happening *inside Jonah*.

Praying the Scriptures

It's important to notice something about Jonah's prayer: he was praying the Scriptures. As you read through Jonah 2, you find echoes of many other passages of Old Testament Scripture (we will look at some of these below). Praying the Scriptures back to the Lord is a beautiful form of prayer. If you have trouble praying for any length of time, and you'd like your time alone with God to be richer and deeper, I encourage you to pray the Scriptures.

A good friend of mine was a great prayer warrior (he has since gone to be with the Lord). People would ask him, "How is it possible for you to pray for an hour and more?" He would answer, "That's simple. I don't do all the talking."

There are two ways we can let God have His say in our prayers. One way is by pausing and listening for His voice speaking to us in the stillness. Another is by praying the Scriptures. We can read or recite His Word, and we can pray God's thoughts from His Word as if they were our own thoughts—we can think God's thoughts after Him.

That is what Jonah did. Out of his watery grave, he prayed the Scriptures back to God. Whenever you are in the belly of the beast, and you don't know how you should pray, pray the Scriptures. Pray His promises: "Lord, You promised that I can cast all my cares on You, for You care for me. You promised that You would carry my grief and sorrows. You promised to give me a garment of praise in place of my garment of sorrow. You promised to give me joy instead of ashes. You promised that You would never leave me nor forsake me. You told me not to fear, because You are with me. You promised to strengthen me and help me, to uphold me with Your right hand. You promised never to give me a spirit of fear but a Spirit of power and love and self-control."

Have you, like Jonah, forsaken God's call on your life? Is God trying to get your attention? Then come to Him in a spirit of contrition and confession, claiming His promise that if you confess your sins, He is faithful and just to forgive your sins and cleanse you from all unrighteousness.

Four Features of Jonah's Prayer

Jonah's prayer is a model prayer for anyone going through a stormy trial. It doesn't matter whether our actions caused the storm or whether we are innocent victims of the storm. Jonah's prayer is a powerful reminder that, even if we forsake God, He never forsakes us. Even though Jonah was on the run from God, he could not escape the loving embrace of God's arms. He had been running, running, running. Finally, he ended up in a place where he could run no longer—the belly of the fish. He couldn't run, couldn't move, and couldn't breathe, yet the Lord granted him enough breath with which to *pray*.

This horrifying, hot, wet, stinking digestive organ of a great sea creature becomes Jonah's prayer chapel. Here in this terrifying place, in this claustrophobic situation, Jonah is forced to stop, consider, and pour out his heart to the Lord.

When everything in life is going well—when our health is good, when we are blessed with abundant possessions, when our buying power knows no bounds—our prayers often become, at best, just a polite nod to the Lord and nothing more. But as soon as trouble strikes—the doctor tells us about a suspicious mass, our son or daughter is arrested on a serious criminal charge, a natural disaster comes out of nowhere and wipes out everything we have—our prayers radically change. They become urgent, anxious, emotional, and frantic, even panicky. We plead with God for mercy.

There are four features of Jonah's prayer that we would do well to understand and emulate in our own times of prayer:

Jonah's prayer was probingly honest.
Jonah's prayer was penitently genuine.
Jonah's prayer was filled with praise.
Jonah's prayer claimed the promises of God.

Let's look at each of these features of Jonah's prayer and apply these lessons to our own lives.

Jonah's Prayer Was Probingly Honest

The prayer of Jonah opens with absolute honesty and with Jonah's recognition that he has brought this horrifying imprisonment on himself:

From inside the fish Jonah prayed to the LORD his God. He said:

> "In my distress I called to the LORD,
> and he answered me.
> From deep in the realm of the dead I called for help,
> and you listened to my cry.
> You hurled me into the depths,
> into the very heart of the seas,
> and the currents swirled about me;
> all your waves and breakers
> swept over me.
> I said, 'I have been banished
> from your sight;
> yet I will look again
> toward your holy temple.'
> The engulfing waters threatened me,
> the deep surrounded me;
> seaweed was wrapped around my head.
> To the roots of the mountains I sank down;
> the earth beneath barred me in forever.
> But you, LORD my God,
> brought my life up from the pit." (Jon. 2:1–6)

It's important to understand the language of the Old Testament as we read Jonah's prayer. When we hear Jonah say, "You hurled me into the depths . . . all your waves and breakers swept over me" (v. 3), we might mistake Jonah's meaning and think he is pointing a finger of blame at God. But Jonah was not blaming God. He was not accusing God of injustice or vindictiveness.

Jonah, like all the saints of the Old Testament, believed in the total sovereignty of God over all things. They believed that God had a moral right to control His entire creation as He saw fit. Even the consequences of human disobedience were acknowledged to be under God's control.

You may recall that after King Saul repeatedly disobeyed God, we find this statement in 1 Samuel 16:14: "Now the Spirit of the LORD had departed from Saul, and an evil spirit from the LORD tormented him." Did the Lord send an evil spirit to torment King Saul? Does God send evil spirits to torment human beings? No, Saul's torment was a direct and natural consequence of the departure of the Holy Spirit from Saul. Through his disobedience, Saul brought this consequence on himself. Saul himself invited this evil spirit into his life. But in the language of the Old Testament, even the evil spirit is said to be "from the LORD" because God is sovereign over all things, even evil spirits.

For a half century or so, our nation has gone the way of Saul. We have expelled God from the schoolhouse to the courthouse, from Wall Street to Main Street, from our public lives to our private lives. And the inevitable consequence of expelling God from our lives is that evil spirits will rush in to fill the vacuum. Does this mean that God, in an active, deliberate, vindictive fashion, sent those evil spirits as a punishment? No, but an Old Testament prophet would have said, "Yes, God has sent those evil spirits. He is sovereign, and He controls the consequences of our actions." That is the language of the Bible. That was the way the Old Testament saints affirmed the absolute sovereignty of God.

In the opening lines of his prayer, Jonah does not accuse God of unfairness. He is not maligning God as people are inclined to do today. He is honestly saying, "Lord, I sinned, and I received the just consequences of my sin. This is what

I had coming to me. I know my sin has brought me to this place. And Lord, I know you are dealing with me, a sinner, in a loving and merciful way."

There's something else we need to see in the opening verses of this prayer: Jonah does not try to explain his misery nor parade his painful circumstances in a bid for pity. He is not trying to paint a picture of his wretched circumstances with all the gory details. Why? Because Jonah is done rationalizing his sins, explaining his bad choices, excusing himself, and blaming others. Jonah realizes he's not qualified to be an advisor and consultant to God.

Jonah recognizes that, through his own sin and rebellion, he has been banished from God's sight, engulfed in the waters, and buried in the depths. How shall he ever again behold the Lord's temple? How shall he ever again worship God with all his heart? Through his own spiritual defection, Jonah has cut himself off from everything that mattered to him. In this probing prayer, he does not spare himself but acknowledges to God that he deserves these consequences, and he bitterly regrets the choices he has made.

Jonah's Prayer Was Penitently Genuine

Penitence is a word we don't hear very often anymore. It's an old English word that means "repentance." From the word *penitence* we get the word *penitentiary*, a prison. The purpose of prison was to make the prisoners stop and take a good hard look at their lives and to come to a place of repentance or penitence.

Jonah was imprisoned in the digestive tract of a giant sea creature, and Jonah's prison had served its purpose. He was deeply, authentically penitent. If he ever got out of that watery prison, he would turn his life in a new direction. In this prayer, Jonah was saying, in effect, "I know that my disobedience brought me here, and that only obedience is going to get me out of here."

Why is this important? Many people feel sorrow and remorse after their disobedience, yet they never repent, they never change direction. It's as if they were driving down the freeway and, realizing they had missed their exit, they kept on going in the same direction, hoping to reach their destination. A refusal to repent when you're moving in the wrong direction will never get you to your destination, either on the freeway or in life. To be penitent means you get off the freeway, turn around, go back and find the right road, and proceed in a new direction.

Repentance is not a feeling. Repentance is an action. Many people feel remorse about their sin. They feel regret. They feel anxious and disturbed. They wish they had never gotten involved in that pattern of sin. They are ashamed. Their guilt gnaws at them. But none of these feelings constitutes repentance. If you feel miserable and guilty but continue in your sin, you have not made a U-turn, you have not changed direction, and you have not repented. Until you take action, all that marinating in sorrow and guilt is meaningless.

Jonah makes a powerful statement in Jonah 2:8: "Those who cling to worthless idols turn away from God's love for them." When you allow idols to dominate you and deter you from serving God, you have walled yourself off from God's love. You are forfeiting the blessings He wants to give you. The blessings of the Lord can only be yours when you say, "I will live my life as a sacrifice to You, Lord; nothing else in this world matters to me."

What are the worthless idols we foolishly cling to? We tend to think of ourselves as enlightened and sophisticated compared to ancient peoples with their "gods" made of stone, metal, and wood. We don't pray to idols, do we? Of course not! This is the twenty-first century!

Well, yes, it is a new era, so we no longer pray to strange little statues. But I see people praying to their idols wherever I go. One of the most common idols people pray to today is the little slab of glass, metal, and silicon chips known as a smartphone. Every day, people bow their heads to them, touch them, mumble to them, listen to them, and seek oracles from them. Vast numbers of people are so addicted to their smartphones they cannot go for more than twenty or thirty minutes at a time without feeling anxious and upset. They crave that little squirt of endorphins in the brain that comes with finding a message from a friend on Instagram or a "like" on their Facebook post. Many people can't spend half an hour at the park with their children or have lunch with friends or spend quiet time with the Lord without stopping to check their phones. Our idolatry of our phones is decreasing our attention spans, impairing our real-world relationships, and turning adults and children into screen-addicted zombies.

Those who understand smartphone and tablet technology best have forbidden their kids to use it. Amazingly, at a time when the late Apple founder Steve Jobs was promoting his new iPad and iPhone products and telling parents that children needed these new electronic "learning tools," he confided to *New York Times* tech reporter Nick Bilton that he shielded his own children from Apple products. "They haven't used [the iPad]," Jobs told Bilton. "We limit how much technology our kids use at home."[1] Jobs understood how addictive these technologies are and how destructive they are to human interaction, even as he reaped hundreds of millions in profits from them.

And every technology that is destructive to human interaction is also destructive to our interaction with God. These are idols. They come between us and God's will for our lives. Yes, a smartphone is an excellent tool if you use it as a tool and not as an idol. I own a smartphone and use it daily. But if you find yourself addicted to it, if you find yourself feeling anxious and incomplete without it, if you find yourself thinking about your phone and obsessing over it when you're without it, you have a problem—and you have an idol.

There are so many idols today I could write a book on the subject. But rather than try to list them, I will simply encourage you to examine your life. Think about the things that you obsess over, about the ways you spend your time, and about the things that come between you and your relationship with God. Ask God to bring to your mind anything that is a barrier between you and Him. Then repent, ask Him to give you the courage to remove that idol from your life, and change direction.

Replace that idol with a realization of God's love for you and the recognition of His blessings in your life. Heed the prayer of Jonah.

Jonah's Prayer Was Filled with Praise

It's one thing to praise God when He has answered your prayer. It's an entirely different level of spiritual maturity if you can praise Him *before* you receive an answer to your prayer. It's one thing to praise God when the sun is shining. It's an entirely different level of spiritual depth if you can praise Him from the belly of the beast.

In verse 9, Jonah prays, "But I, with shouts of grateful praise, will sacrifice to you. What I have vowed I will make good. I will say, 'Salvation comes from the Lord.'"

Jonah had no way of knowing if he would be delivered or if the alimentary canal of that sea creature would be his final resting place. Earlier in his prayer, he spoke of his soul fainting within him, of his utter helplessness and hopelessness. Yet here, Jonah praises God nonetheless.

There is a feature of Jonah's prayer that you and I must not miss: nowhere in this prayer does Jonah ask God to deliver him. Read this prayer again and you will see that he prays, from beginning to end, *as if he has already been delivered*. He does not say, "Lord, listen to my cry!" He says, "You *listened* to my cry," past tense (v. 2, emphasis added). He does not say, "Lord, rescue me from this pit!" He says, "You, Lord my God, *brought* my life up from the pit," past tense (v. 6, emphasis added).

Jonah doesn't ask for anything in this prayer. Instead, it is a prayer of thanksgiving for the deliverance Jonah expects to receive. He prays as if the rescue has already taken place. He doesn't withhold his praise until God delivers him. He immediately begins praising God in the midst of his crisis, in the midst of the stink and the stomach acids of the fish, in the midst of the heat and the slime and the rotting seaweed and fish food that clings to him. Could you praise God in the midst of that situation?

This is a gift and an art and a spiritual discipline that we need to cultivate as Christians—the ability to praise God in a crisis. I steadfastly believe that praising God in the midst of tough times is truly the secret to victory.

Acts 16 tells us that Paul and Silas were singing hymns and praising God, not in the air-conditioned comfort of a megachurch auditorium but in a cold, stinking Roman prison cell in Philippi. They had been stripped, beaten with rods, and flogged within an inch of their lives. They were bleeding and unable to sleep because of their pain. The guards had fastened their feet in stocks. Yet they were singing and praising the Lord in the midst of their suffering.

Then, around midnight, as they were still praying and singing to God, the earth shook, the cell doors swung open, and the chains fell off all the prisoners. The jailer, knowing he would be executed if even one prisoner escaped, was ready to fall on his sword when Paul shouted to him, "Don't harm yourself! We are all here!" (v. 28).

Paul shared the gospel with the jailer and led him to the Lord. God is glorified and souls are drawn into His kingdom when we praise God in the midst of tough times.

I have sometimes heard people say, "I can't do that. I don't have anything to praise God for. I don't have anything to be thankful for." Really? You don't have life and breath? You don't have anyone in your life who loves you? You don't have any blessings of food, comfort, medical care, books to read, God's Word to meditate on, Christian messages to listen to, nothing, no blessings whatsoever?

My guess is that, if you think hard enough, you can find some blessing in your life to praise God for. And once you begin to praise Him, your songs and shouts of praise will open your prison door and set off an earthquake of blessing for the people around you. Praise unlocks the door to blessing. Jonah's prayer was rich in authentic praise to God.

Jonah's Prayer Claimed the Promises of God

Again and again in this passage, Jonah prays the promises of God as they have been given throughout the Old Testament Scriptures, especially in the book of Psalms. In verse 2, Jonah says, "In my distress I called to the Lord, and he answered me. From deep in the realm of the dead I called for help, and you listened to my cry." Compare this triumphant claim in Jonah's prayer with the promise of Psalm 18:4–6:

> The cords of death entangled me;
> the torrents of destruction overwhelmed me.
> The cords of the grave coiled around me;
> the snares of death confronted me.
>
> In my distress I called to the Lord;
> I cried to my God for help.
> From his temple he heard my voice;
> my cry came before him, into his ears.

Or the promise of Psalm 86:13:

> For great is your love toward me;
> you have delivered me from the depths,
> from the realm of the dead.

Or the promise of Psalm 120:1:

> I call on the Lord in my distress,
> and he answers me.

Or the promise of Lamentations 3:53–56:

They tried to end my life in a pit
    and threw stones at me;
the waters closed over my head,
    and I thought I was about to perish.

I called on your name, Lord,
    from the depths of the pit.
You heard my plea: "Do not close your ears
    to my cry for relief."

In verse 4, Jonah says, "I have been banished from your sight; yet I will look again toward your holy temple." Compare Jonah's prayer with the promise of Psalm 31:22:

In my alarm I said,
    "I am cut off from your sight!"
Yet you heard my cry for mercy
    when I called to you for help.

Or the promise of Psalm 5:7:

But I, by your great love,
    can come into your house;
in reverence I bow down
    toward your holy temple.

In verse 6, Jonah says, "To the roots of the mountains I sank down; the earth beneath barred me in forever. But you, Lord my God, brought my life up from the pit." Compare Jonah's prayer in this verse with the promise of Psalm 30:3:

You, Lord, brought me up from the realm of the
    dead;
    you spared me from going down to the pit.

Or the promise of Isaiah 38:17:

> Surely it was for my benefit
>   that I suffered such anguish.
> In your love you kept me
>   from the pit of destruction;
> you have put all my sins
>   behind your back.

In verse 7, Jonah says, "When my life was ebbing away, I remembered you, LORD, and my prayer rose to you, to your holy temple." Compare Jonah's prayer in this verse with the promise of Psalm 18:6:

> In my distress I called to the LORD;
>   I cried to my God for help.
> From his temple he heard my voice;
>   my cry came before him, into his ears.

Perhaps the most important of all the promises Jonah claims is found in verse 9 of his prayer: "But I, with shouts of grateful praise, will sacrifice to you. What I have vowed I will make good. I will say, 'Salvation comes from the LORD.'" Compare this triumphant statement in Jonah's prayer with the blessed promise of Psalm 3:8:

> From the LORD comes deliverance.
> May your blessing be on your people.

Salvation comes from the Lord. We are helpless to save ourselves. We have no righteousness to offer Him. We have nothing to offer God but the blessings He has poured into our lives by the riches of His grace—blessings and riches that were already His to begin with.

Jonah vowed to sacrifice to God with shouts of grateful praise. Gratitude and praise are all we have to give Him. We cannot come to God saying, "Look at all the good things I have done for You, Lord, at all the sacrifices I have made for You. Look at everything You owe me, Lord." No, we owe Him everything, and He owes us nothing.

So we come to God, offering Him our sacrifices, acknowledging that we have nothing to cling to but His grace, nothing to claim but His promises, nothing to brag about but His extravagant, unconditional love. When we approach Him in the spirit that Jonah demonstrates here, we can only be amazed. God loves to fulfill His promises to those who faithfully cling to them.

The last verse of Jonah 2 tells us what happened after Jonah prayed this prayer: "And the LORD commanded the fish, and it vomited Jonah onto dry land" (v. 10).

When Jonah prayed from the belly of the fish, he didn't know *how* God would deliver him or *when* God would deliver him. He didn't even know *if* God would deliver him alive, safe and sound, on dry land, or if his deliverance would take the form of physical death. He simply trusted that God, in His own sovereign way and by His own sovereign choice, would deliver him from the belly of that fish.

A Prayer from the Pit of Despair

On May 26, 2013, a tugboat, *Jascon-4*, with a crew of twelve, was attempting to stabilize an oil tanker docked at a Chevron drilling platform in the Atlantic Ocean twelve miles off the coast of Nigeria. The seas were rough and churning. At 4:30 a.m., a sudden swell severed the tow cable and capsized the tugboat, causing it to sink to the bottom of the sea, settling upside down at a depth of one hundred feet. Eleven of the crew drowned within minutes.

Only the ship's cook, Harrison Odjegba Okene, was still alive. He had found an air-filled space about four feet in height that enabled him to breathe. Dressed only in his undershorts, he fashioned a makeshift bed so that he could keep his body out of the freezing water that filled most of the boat. Had he remained in the water, he would have died of hypothermia within hours. For nourishment, he found a single bottle of Coca-Cola. To dispel the darkness, he found a life vest with two flashlights attached.

He hoped for, but didn't expect, a rescue attempt. As he waited, he prayed—and he listened to the sounds of sharks entering other chambers of the capsized tugboat, devouring the bodies of his drowned shipmates.

Harrison Okene waited in that overturned hold for sixty hours—the better part of three days. In fact, his ordeal lasted about as long as Jonah's. His air should not have held out that long, but being trapped so deep in the ocean actually worked in his favor. He had a little more than two hundred cubic feet of air to breathe, about an eighteen-hour supply at surface pressures. But the immense pressure at the bottom of the ocean condensed more than sixty hours' worth of oxygen into that small bubble of life. The water that half filled the compartment he was trapped in helped absorb the carbon dioxide gas he exhaled before it reached lethal levels.

On the third day of his captivity in the overturned tugboat, he heard noises—bumping and scraping sounds—from the hull. Salvage divers had descended to the wrecked tugboat to retrieve the bodies of the dead sailors.

They had already retrieved four bodies when one diver felt something brush the back of his neck. Freaked out, the diver turned and the lamp on his face mask illuminated a hand in the dark, murky water. The diver shouted, "Corpse, corpse, corpse!" into his microphone.

Then the hand, which protruded from an opening in the hull, reached out toward the diver's face. The diver freaked out again, shouting, "It's alive, it's alive, it's alive!"

For the diver, it was as if he had seen a ghost. There was no way anyone could still be alive on the third day in the belly of that boat. But the diver swam into the boat and came up in the chamber where Harrison Okene waited, and the Nigerian sea cook realized he was going to be delivered from his watery tomb.

The divers moved him into a decompression chamber and slowly brought him to the surface to prevent him from getting the bends from nitrogen bubbles in his bloodstream. When he was finally able to step out of the chamber and onto the deck of the rescue ship, Harrison Okene saw that it was night and the sky was full of stars. He thought his ordeal had lasted twenty-four hours and was astonished to find he had been at the bottom of the ocean for nearly *three times* as long.

Though Harrison Okene wasn't trapped in the belly of a big fish, he probably came as close to a Jonah-like experience as any human being has ever lived to tell about. And while he was in the belly of that tugboat, he responded very much as Jonah did. He prayed.

"All around me," he later told a reporter, "was just black. . . . I was crying and calling on Jesus to rescue me, I prayed so hard. I was so hungry and thirsty and cold and I was just praying to see some kind of light."[2] God answered that prayer, and Harrison Okene did see the light of God's deliverance.

Whatever pit of despair you find yourself in, whatever waters may threaten to engulf you, whatever darkness may surround you, remember the prayer of Jonah. Pray a prayer of praise and gratitude for the light and rescue that is to come. Remind yourself, "Salvation comes from the LORD!"

6

HABAKKUK

A Prayer of Complaint,
a Prayer of Rejoicing

Habakkuk 3:1–19

William Cowper (1731–1800) was an English poet and hymn writer. One of his closest friends was John Newton, the former slave trader who wrote "Amazing Grace." Cowper struggled with depression and mental illness throughout his life. He was haunted by a persistent notion that God didn't love him and had condemned him despite his desire to follow Christ. Though we have many assurances in the Bible of God's love and forgiveness when we receive Christ as our Lord and Savior, Cowper battled this strange obsession for years.

He attempted suicide several times and was institutionalized for insanity from 1763 to 1765. After his release, he took comfort in immersing himself in prayer, Bible reading, and long conversations with other Christians. Yet from time to time he was still plagued by doubts, and those doubts would fill him with suicidal thoughts.

One night, as London lay shrouded in an impenetrable fog, Cowper again fell into a deep depression and decided to take his life. He called a coachman to drive him to London Bridge. There he planned to leap into the Thames River and drown his tortured soul. The coachman drove Cowper through the fog in search of the bridge but soon became lost.

Finally, Cowper told the coachman to let him off, and he would find his destination on foot. Cowper stepped out of the coach and tried to get his bearings. As the coachman pulled away, Cowper made an astonishing discovery: he was standing on the street in front of his own home. The lost and bewildered coachman had driven in circles and brought Cowper back to the place from which he had started.

Cowper realized that only God's hand could have guided him to his own doorstep. Cowper had been brooding, thinking God didn't love him, but here was proof that God loved him far more than he knew. This was God's way of reaching into the dark fog of Cowper's depression and saying, "I love you." William Cowper decided to live for God instead of dying in self-pity. He went to his desk that night and began composing one of his best-loved hymns:

> God moves in a mysterious way
> His wonders to perform;
> He plants His footsteps in the sea
> And rides upon the storm.
>
> Deep in unfathomable mines
> Of never failing skill
> He treasures up His bright designs
> And works His sovereign will.

Ye fearful saints, fresh courage take;
The clouds ye so much dread
Are big with mercy and shall break
In blessings on your head.

I don't know why God allows some of His saints to struggle year after year with doubts, depression, and mental illness. I don't know why some, like William Cowper, struggle year after year with unanswered prayer over deep spiritual and emotional agonies. But I do know that God loves them.

In those times when our prayers seem to go unanswered, when God seems to delay, when our pleas to God seem to bounce off leaden skies, or when we receive an answer to prayer that is the opposite of what we hoped for, we struggle and sink into depression.

Or we become angry with God.

Or we develop a distant and cold love toward God.

Or we give up praying altogether.

As we turn to the prayer of the prophet Habakkuk, we're about to see a very different response to unanswered prayer. We're going to see Habakkuk take the trial of unanswered prayer and turn it into an opportunity to grow in his faith: to grow in his knowledge of God and to grow in intimacy with God in prayer.

We will see Habakkuk ask God, in effect, "What do You want me to learn from this? How can I learn to pray in greater alignment with Your will? Lord, teach me to trust You more." In the prayer of Habakkuk, we find a model of prayer that will protect us from the disillusionment, discouragement, and depression that so often accompany God's delays in answering our prayers.

A Prophet of Mystery and Influence

The Bible gives us several reasons why our prayers sometimes seem to go unanswered. The Epistle of James tells us that sometimes we pray and receive no answer because, deep down, we really don't expect an answer to prayer:

> But when you ask, you must believe and not doubt, because the one who doubts is like a wave of the sea, blown and tossed by the wind. That person should not expect to receive anything from the Lord. (James 1:6–7)

And in Luke 18, the Lord tells the story of the persistent widow and the unjust judge. The widow nags and badgers the judge into giving her justice. This judge (who is nothing like God, who deeply loves us and *wants* to hear our prayers!) gives this woman what she demands simply because she is so aggravatingly persistent. More often than we realize, the delays in God's answers to our prayers may simply be the result of our lack of persistence in prayer.

I once heard of a woman who called the opera house and said she had lost an expensive diamond bracelet during the evening's performance. The manager asked her to stay on the line while he and his staff conducted a thorough search. After about fifteen minutes of searching, they found the bracelet. The manager went back to the phone, only to find that she had lost patience and hung up. He didn't know how to contact her.

Of course, God knows how to find us, but if we are not willing to be persistent in prayer, what reason have we given Him to answer our prayers? God delights in answering our prayers, but He wants us to desire an intense and intimate relationship with Him. That means we must be willing to persist with Him in prayer. We see a great Old Testament example of persisting in prayer in the three chapters of the book of Habakkuk.

Almost nothing is known about the prophet Habakkuk—where he was born, when he lived, when he died. Even the meaning of his name is a mystery. There is no Hebrew word that seems to be a root word for Habakkuk. His name does not appear anywhere else in the Old Testament. Despite the mysteries surrounding the prophet Habakkuk, he had a profound influence on Christian writers and on the early Protestant reformers, especially Martin Luther.

Historical clues within the book of Habakkuk suggest that he lived during the reign of Israel's King Jehoiakim, when the Babylonian Empire was on the rise but before the Babylonians came to lay siege to Jerusalem. The book is divided into three chapters, each with a distinct theme. Habakkuk 1 consists of a dialogue between God and the prophet Habakkuk. Chapter 2 is a pronouncement of doom against unfaithful Israel. And Habakkuk 3 is the prophet's great prayer, which is written as a song or psalm and was undoubtedly put to music and performed during temple worship.

The central theme of the book of Habakkuk focuses on the prophet's effort to grow from a place of doubt and impatience with God to a place of complete trust in Him, despite God's apparent delay in answering prayer. Initially, the prophet Habakkuk is amazingly bold, almost to the point of being disrespectful to God. In the first chapter, he complains about God's delays in judging the violence and injustice in the world:

> How long, Lord, must I call for help,
>   but you do not listen?
> Or cry out to you, "Violence!"
>   but you do not save?

Why do you make me look at injustice?
  Why do you tolerate wrongdoing?
Destruction and violence are before me;
  there is strife, and conflict abounds.
Therefore the law is paralyzed,
  and justice never prevails.
The wicked hem in the righteous,
  so that justice is perverted. (vv. 2–4)

God responds to Habakkuk's complaint, and the prophet was undoubtedly shocked and horrified by what he heard. God says:

Look at the nations and watch—
  and be utterly amazed.
For I am going to do something in your days
  that you would not believe,
  even if you were told.
I am raising up the Babylonians,
  that ruthless and impetuous people,
who sweep across the whole earth
  to seize dwellings not their own. (vv. 5–6)

God is answering Habakkuk's prayer, but not in the way Habakkuk expects. God tells him, in so many words, "I heard your prayer, and I will respond to your pleas—but not yet. Right now, I'm raising up a pagan nation, a brutal and blood-thirsty people, the Babylonians. They will come and take Israel into exile in Babylon."

I suspect that when Habakkuk heard these words, he said to himself, *What have I done? That's not the answer I was looking for! I didn't want my own people to be conquered and led off into a foreign land. That's not what I was praying for! How can a merciful God do such a thing? How can a loving God allow wicked people to punish His own people?*

In the second chapter, we see the Lord's response to Habakkuk's second complaint:

> Write down the revelation
>   and make it plain on tablets
>   so that a herald may run with it.
> For the revelation awaits an appointed time;
>   it speaks of the end
>   and will not prove false.
> Though it linger, wait for it;
>   it will certainly come
>   and will not delay.
>
> See, the enemy is puffed up;
>   his desires are not upright—
>   but the righteous person will live by his faithfulness.
>   (vv. 2–4)

Here, the Lord commands Habakkuk to write down the revelation God is about to give him and to make it so simple and plain that anyone can understand it. This revelation is a warning of approaching destruction, the impending Babylonian conquest and exile. The pagan Babylonians are arising in the East. They are arrogant, wicked, and violent, and God is going to use this ungodly nation to accomplish a godly purpose. He is going to use Babylon to discipline the unrighteous, rebellious, idolatrous Israelites.

God is saying, "Times may be bad now, spiritually speaking, but there are worse days ahead for the Jewish nation. Yes, I will use Babylon for my purposes. Yes, I will carry out my repeated warnings against the idol worshipers and lawbreakers in Israel. Yes, I will deal with the arrogant, the unjust, and the unrighteous. Yes, I will judge the wicked. But I will do so at a time of My choosing."

Not everyone in Israel will be destroyed or taken captive by the Babylonians. The righteous will live by faith. God will protect the faithful. No matter what happens, no matter what the future brings, no matter what suffering lies ahead, whether the economy rises or falls, whether politicians behave righteously or corruptly, God is in control of history. He is on His throne. He will not forsake the faithful.

Implicit in God's answer to Habakkuk's questions about unanswered prayer are some crucial lessons for Habakkuk's life—and ours. God is telling Habakkuk and us that when we see strange, momentous events happening around us, when the world seems to be going mad, when all the foundations and structures of society seem to be crumbling and collapsing, we will be tempted to ask, as Habakkuk did, "God, how long must we cry out to You for help? Are You listening? Don't You care about the violence and injustice and wrongdoing all around us?"

God is telling us that we are asking the wrong questions. He wants us to know that when we see these strange things happening, we shouldn't complain. Instead, we should ask ourselves, "What is God trying to teach me through these events? Is there something in my own life that I need to correct? Is there sin in my life that I need to deal with? Is my faith weak and immature, and do I need to grow in my faith? Instead of blaming God in the midst of these crises, shouldn't I be praising God instead?"

When God delays in answering our prayers, there is always a good reason. As we become mature in the faith, we realize we can trust the delays of God to be for our good and for His glory. When God delays in answering our prayers, it might be because He is dealing with selfishness in our hearts, in the hearts of those we are praying for, or in the heart of the nation we are praying for. God might be dealing with arrogance, rebelliousness, or sin in our lives. God might be delaying in answering our prayers because He is purifying His church and preparing His people for greater things to come. He is working out both judgment and righteousness and weaving all these events into His eternal plan—His grand purpose for human history.

An Instructive Prayer

Now we come to the great psalm-like prayer of Habakkuk, which spans the entire third and final chapter of the book.

> Lord, I have heard of your fame;
> > I stand in awe of your deeds, Lord.
> Repeat them in our day,
> > in our time make them known;
> > in wrath remember mercy.
>
> God came from Teman,
> > the Holy One from Mount Paran.
> His glory covered the heavens
> > and his praise filled the earth.
> His splendor was like the sunrise;
> > rays flashed from his hand,
> > where his power was hidden.
> Plague went before him;
> > pestilence followed his steps.

He stood, and shook the earth;
    he looked, and made the nations tremble.
The ancient mountains crumbled
    and the age-old hills collapsed—
    but he marches on forever.
I saw the tents of Cushan in distress,
    the dwellings of Midian in anguish.

Were you angry with the rivers, LORD?
    Was your wrath against the streams?
Did you rage against the sea
    when you rode your horses
    and your chariots to victory?
You uncovered your bow,
    you called for many arrows.
You split the earth with rivers;
    the mountains saw you and writhed.
Torrents of water swept by;
    the deep roared
    and lifted its waves on high.

Sun and moon stood still in the heavens
    at the glint of your flying arrows,
    at the lightning of your flashing spear.
In wrath you strode through the earth
    and in anger you threshed the nations.
You came out to deliver your people,
    to save your anointed one.
You crushed the leader of the land of wickedness,
    you stripped him from head to foot.
With his own spear you pierced his head
    when his warriors stormed out to scatter us,
gloating as though about to devour
    the wretched who were in hiding.

You trampled the sea with your horses,
    churning the great waters.

I heard and my heart pounded,
    my lips quivered at the sound;
decay crept into my bones,
    and my legs trembled.
Yet I will wait patiently for the day of calamity
    to come on the nation invading us.
Though the fig tree does not bud
    and there are no grapes on the vines,
though the olive crop fails
    and the fields produce no food,
though there are no sheep in the pen
    and no cattle in the stalls,
yet I will rejoice in the LORD,
    I will be joyful in God my Savior.

The Sovereign LORD is my strength;
    he makes my feet like the feet of a deer,
    he enables me to tread on the heights.

The prophet Habakkuk begins by saying, "LORD, I have heard of your fame; I stand in awe of your deeds, LORD. Repeat them in our day, in our time make them known; in wrath remember mercy" (v. 2). What "deeds" does Habakkuk refer to?

Habakkuk begins his prayer by asking for revival. He says, in effect, "Lord, the Scriptures are filled with the mighty deeds that You have done in the past. I pray that You would repeat these mighty works in our own time. Make Your power and glory known among our people today, so that we will have a resurgence of worship and praise to You in our own time."

There is never a wrong time to pray for revival. I am encouraged to see many people praying and asking the Lord for revival in America in the twenty-first century. Habakkuk was praying for revival in his own time, and it is a great prayer, the kind of prayer every believer should pray.

Did God want Israel to experience revival in that day? Absolutely! Does God want to see His church revived today? Without question! Then why did God delay in answering Habakkuk's prayer? Habakkuk found this question extremely baffling. And why is He delaying in answering our prayer for revival today? Why do our prayers for revival seem to go unanswered?

I think the reason for God's delay in reviving the church today is the same reason God delayed in answering the prayer of Habakkuk for Israel.

Israel in the Time of Habakkuk

To fully understand Habakkuk's prayer, we need to understand the background and the events of the book of Habakkuk. At the time of Habakkuk's prophetic ministry, idolatry was rampant and sin was epidemic in Israel. The people of Israel had compromised the pure and holy worship of God by importing into their religion the idols and abominable practices of the surrounding pagan cultures. God had told the people through Moses that they must have no other gods before Him, yet they had demoted the one true God, the maker of heaven and earth, to a position of chief deity in a pantheon of many deities.

The Israelites of Habakkuk's day would tell you, "Oh, we haven't abandoned God! See? We worship Him right alongside all these other gods we have adopted." That's like a husband saying to his wife, "Oh, I haven't abandoned you! I haven't betrayed you! Sure, I have all these other girlfriends, but you're the one I'm married to, you're the one I love most!" This is an apt analogy because throughout the Old Testament, God pictures idolatry as spiritual infidelity and adultery.

The people of Israel in Habakkuk's day were still "married" to the Lord, to Yahweh, the God of Abraham, Isaac, and Jacob, but their commitment to Him was halfhearted at best. Their love for Yahweh had grown cold. They still went to the temple and followed the rituals prescribed by the law of Moses. But their hearts weren't in it. Why? Because their feelings of love and worship and religious ardor were no longer reserved for God alone but were divided among many false, demonic gods, some of which demanded hideous sacrificial rites, including the sacrifice of children.

The Israelites also worshiped prosperity, selfishness, fertility, and unrestrained sexuality. They claimed to believe in God, but they worshiped the self. Through their idolatry and spiritual adultery, the Israelites had earned God's wrath. That is why Habakkuk prays, "In wrath remember mercy."

Habakkuk's prayer for revival was urgently needed.

Learning to Pray Effectively

Three features of Habakkuk's prayer in chapter 3 stand out and are worth noting and incorporating into our own prayers to the Lord:

Habakkuk's humility before God
Habakkuk's adoration of God
Habakkuk's focus on God's work

Habakkuk's Humility before God

The first feature of effective prayer is humility. We see Habakkuk's humility before God when he says, "LORD, I have heard of your fame; I stand in awe of your deeds" (3:2). These words are in marked contrast to the opening lines of the book of Habakkuk. In chapter 1, the prophet Habakkuk seems to be lecturing the Lord: "How long, LORD, must I call for help, but you do not listen? Or cry out to you, 'Violence!' but you do not save?" (1:2).

But now Habakkuk has grown deeper and more mature in his faith. Now instead of lecturing God because of unanswered prayer, Habakkuk stands in awe of God's mighty works.

I once watched a television preacher who put on quite a performance. He strutted around the platform like a peacock, shouting a prayer in which he ordered Jesus around, telling Jesus that He had to do this and He had to do that, and He had to do it in this exact way, and He had to do it *now*! I literally felt like weeping for this man and for all his viewers who were being led astray by this arrogant approach to prayer.

Since when does the Creator of the universe take orders from us? God *responds* to humility in prayer. God is *honored* by humility in prayer. God is *moved* by humility in prayer. And humility means we recognize that God is God, and we are not. God knows whether He should say yes to our prayers. He knows when He should respond instantly and when He should delay. Ordering God around in prayer—acting like He is a genie from Aladdin's lamp who exists only to do our bidding—is sheer arrogance and hubris. Barking orders at God is way above our spiritual pay grade.

When Habakkuk started this dialogue with God, he was much like that strutting peacock of a TV preacher, demanding that God justify Himself and explain what's taking so long with those answers to prayer he ordered. But something happened in Habakkuk's life between chapters 1 and 3. He learned to take his mind off himself and his own problems. He learned to take his mind off the rebellious Israelites and the godless Babylonians and the international strife in the world.

Habakkuk learned to focus on God alone.

As long as Habakkuk operated on a merely human level, comparing the unrighteousness of the Israelites with the ungodliness of the Babylonians and focusing on the violence and injustice of this world, he had an unhealthy view of God. He was looking at God through the wrong end of the telescope and saw an unjust, unwise, and unrighteous God who let world events get out of control. The God Habakkuk saw took too long to answer prayer and needed to explain Himself and defend Himself to the prophet.

But once Habakkuk stopped reading all the bad news in the newspaper about worsening tensions between Israel and Babylon, once he took his eyes off who was up and who was down, who was in and who was out, once he fixed his gaze squarely on the righteousness and majesty of God, everything else faded away into insignificance.

I believe that many of us in the church are like the Pharisee who went to the temple and prayed, "God, I thank you that I am not like other people—robbers, evildoers, adulterers" (Luke 18:11). When we approach God in prayer, we often think, *Lord, in comparison to Mr. Smith over there, in comparison to Mrs. Jones over there, I'm not all that bad. Please grade me on a curve, and please answer my prayers.* This is not the basis on which God answers prayer. We can't come to God and hold out our own paltry righteousness to Him and say, "This is why I deserve to have my prayers answered. Lord, please answer my prayers according to these filthy rags of righteousness I hold in my hands."

We are often like the person who passed an anonymous note up to evangelist R. A. Torrey as he sat on the platform, preparing to preach. The note read:

> I have been praying for a long time for something that I am confident is according to God's will, but I do not get it. . . . I have been Superintendent in the Sunday school for twenty-five years, and an elder in the church for twenty years; and yet God does not answer my prayer and I cannot understand it. Can you explain it to me?

Torrey used the anonymous note to make an important point in his sermon. He said that the person who wrote the note mistakenly thought that being a Sunday school super-intendent or church elder for years placed God under an obligation to answer those prayers. Was this person really praying in God's name, according to God's will? No. Torrey concluded, "He is really praying in his own name."[1]

How we approach God will determine the effectiveness of our prayers. We must approach Him in an attitude of humility, not one of entitlement or self-sufficiency. If God is going to send revival to the church today, it won't be because of how faithful we have been. No, it will be because of how merciful He is.

Habakkuk tried to approach God with his demands, and God had to set him straight. Habakkuk learned humility in prayer.

Habakkuk's Adoration of God

The second feature of effective prayer that we find in the prayer of Habakkuk is adoration. Biblical adoration is an aspect of worship. Adoration is our expression of love for God through prayer, praise, songs, and acts of service and worship. When we feel and express adoration for God, we fulfill the Great Commandment: "Jesus replied: 'Love the Lord your God with all your heart and with all your soul and with all your mind'" (Matt. 22:37). When we pray, do we express our adoration for Him? Do we express to Him that we love Him with all our heart, soul, and mind? Or do we just present our wish list to Him, our list of urgent needs and wants? I don't want to give the impression that we are wrong to present our requests to God in prayer. Jesus taught us to ask of God, who wants to give good gifts to His children. But if our wish list is the sum total of our prayer life, then we have a weak and anemic prayer life. There is so much more to prayer than asking God to meet our needs.

Emotions of awe and adoration are woven throughout Habakkuk 3. In this prayer, Habakkuk speaks adoringly of God's power, His righteousness, and His deliverance of His people. Habakkuk is in awe of the Lord's deeds, His glory and splendor, His everlasting nature, and the brilliant power of God that eclipses the very sun and moon. Habakkuk is not only amazed at God's power; he is also captivated by God's righteousness. The Lord judges the wicked, threshes the godless nations, and delivers His people from destruction. The Lord is Habakkuk's joy and strength.

Is God our joy and strength as well? Are we in awe of His deeds, His glory and splendor, His righteousness and goodness toward us? Do we love and adore Him for who He is and what He has done in our lives?

A healthy and robust prayer life begins with an understanding of Who God is and what it means to pray to Him. To enter the throne room of God is to adore who He is. To enter the very heart of God is to open our hearts to Him and pour out our love for Him. To worship Him is to recognize that He is worthy of our love and adoration.

Many Christians come to God as a kind of unpleasant obligation. We go through the motions of praising Him and thanking Him, and then we're glad that's over so we can get on with our day. That's not what our relationship with God is supposed to be like.

The psalmist said, "Take delight in the LORD, and he will give you the desires of your heart" (Ps. 37:4). This means that you find *joy* in His presence; you seek out time with Him as you would any treasured friend. This also means that when you are with the Lord, you feel blessed, happy, and excited, and you give Him all your attention. Later, during the day, you think of the time that you spent with Him, and the memory of it brings a smile to your face. It was delightful to be with Him, and you can't wait until your next special time alone with Him.

When you delight in the Lord, you think about Who He is, what He has done for you, what amazing perfection of character He possesses, and what an abundance of mercy and grace He has showered on you. And then, when you pray to Him, you find yourself asking for only those things that delight His heart—that's how much He means to you. Your thoughts and prayers blend and merge with His heart; your heart and His beat as one.

When you pray, ask God to teach you more about Himself and what it means to follow Him. Ask the Holy Spirit to teach you how to delight yourself in the Lord. These are prayers that will always be honored. Learn to adore the Lord in prayer as Habakkuk adored Him. That's a key lesson we learn from the prayer of Habakkuk.

Habakkuk's Focus on God's Work

The third feature of effective prayer is to focus on God's work. Habakkuk prayed that God in His mercy would send a great awakening to Israel. The people of Israel didn't deserve it; they deserved only the destruction that God had repeatedly warned them was coming. But Habakkuk desired that God would bring revival so that His name would be glorified. The word *revival* means to make alive again. To revive something is to make it alive after it has already been dead.

Some people think a revival is when you gather a big crowd in a stadium and sing praises to God. Well, that kind of revival is a good thing, and we need more of it, but that's not what the Bible means by revival. When the spiritually dead become alive through the power of the Holy Spirit, that is true revival and a work of God.

Habakkuk was concerned about the lack of revival in Israel—his own ministry, his own country, his own people—because there was no revival, no life. The Holy Spirit was not moving among the people and bringing this dead nation back to life again. But once he took his eyes off the spiritual deadness of the nation and focused on the awe-inspiring glory of God, he saw even the Babylonian exile as part of God's plan for revival.

History tells us that revival often takes place during the darkest times in the life of a nation. The Protestant Reformation took place in the 1500s during a period of spiritual death and moral corruption that we rightly call the Dark Ages. During that time, Pope Alexander VI had filled the Vatican with his own illegitimate children, and he didn't care who knew it. He would lift those children up before the public as if to boast of his corruption. The popes that followed him—Pope Julius II, Pope Leo X, and others—used the papacy to accumulate wealth and power for themselves. The Roman Catholic Church in Europe was materially rich and morally bankrupt. Ignorance of the Bible was rampant as was pagan superstition. The people worshiped the saints and sought special knowledge and insight from the demon-possessed.

Into this cesspool of spiritual corruption stepped a man named Martin Luther. As a devout and pious priest, he was sickened by the corruption in the church. One day, as he was reading the New Testament, he came across Romans 1:17, one of three verses in the New Testament that quote Habakkuk. Luther read, "For in the gospel the righteousness of God is revealed—a righteousness that is by faith from first to last, just as it is written: 'The righteous will live by faith.'"

Those words struck Luther like a thunderbolt. In a flash of insight, he realized that this was the truth the church had buried under a suffocating pile of ritual and false dogma. *The righteous will live by faith.* And this understanding quickened Luther's spirit and thoroughly converted him to faith in Jesus Christ. He set in motion the Protestant Reformation, which led the world out of the Dark Ages and into an era of biblical enlightenment and evangelism.

Fast-forward two centuries and move across the water to America. There, Jonathan Edwards had succeeded his grandfather as minister of the church in Northampton, Massachusetts. Society was steeped in darkness. Church leaders bickered and fought with each other. Sexual immorality was rampant. The family was breaking down. But a small faithful remnant of people prayed for an awakening from the Holy Spirit. And one of those faithful believers, Jonathan Edwards, became a leader in what is known as the First Great Awakening.

Not long after this movement began in America, a similar movement was born in England. Once again, this revival had its origins in a spiritually dark era in England. Religion in England was staid, formal, and dead. Drunkenness was epidemic, and sexual immorality was so commonplace that children didn't know who their fathers were. God moved in the hearts of three key men—George Whitefield, Charles Wesley, and Charles's brother John Wesley. Their zeal for the gospel and their desire to please God drove them to their knees to pray for England. And God used these three praying, preaching, witnessing men to transform England for Christ.

In New York City in the 1850s, a man named Jeremiah Lanphier distributed handbills announcing that weekly prayer meetings would be held every Wednesday during the noon hour in the Consistory building behind the North Dutch Church at Fulton and William Streets. He set up eleven chairs in the room, then he waited to see who would show up. At his first meeting, hardly anyone came. The following week, there were a few more. The week after that, a few more. He kept inviting, kept praying, and the prayer meeting began to grow.

Soon, the little Consistory building could no longer contain the weekly prayer meetings. The meetings were expanded to other places around the city. Soon, the Wednesday prayer meetings were being held all over Manhattan.

Jeremiah Lanphier was not a preacher; he was a businessman. But God honored his faithful prayer. In every revival in history, people have prayed like Habakkuk: "In wrath remember mercy."

And a prayer for mercy will always move the heart of God.

7

MARY

A Prayer-Song of Praise

Luke 1:46–55

The expectant silence is broken by a trumpet fanfare, a shout of triumph from throats fashioned of brass. Timpani resound! Violins join the chorus! Flute notes flutter in midair! The music exalts and exults.

Then voices, like a choir of angels, join the celebration! "Magnificat!" sing the angelic sopranos. "Magnificat!" reply the angelic tenors.

So begins the *Magnificat in D Major*, an orchestral and choral masterpiece that Johann Sebastian Bach composed in honor of a little prayer said centuries ago by a humble teenage girl in Palestine. It is soaring music. It swells the heart and makes the spine tingle. It touches the soul and brings tears to the eyes.

And yet, as beautiful as Bach's music is, as much as it lifts the soul and quickens the pulse, I think it falls short of the simple heartfelt majesty of the original Magnificat composed by Mary, the mother of Jesus. Mary's Magnificat is a canticle, a hymn of praise to God. The title comes from the first line of the Latin translation: *Magnificat anima mea Dominum*, "My soul magnifies the Lord."

In the Gospel of Luke, Mary goes into the hill country of Judea where her cousin Elizabeth lives. Elizabeth is pregnant with the baby who will grow to be John the Baptist. When Mary and Elizabeth greet each other, Elizabeth's unborn baby leaps within her womb, and Elizabeth says, "Blessed is she who has believed that the Lord would fulfill his promises to her!" (Luke 1:45). Mary then responds with this beautiful canticle of praise to God.

Mary's prayer of praise is one of the most often recited prayers in Christian liturgy. Among Protestants, the Magnificat is frequently sung or read during the Advent season. It is sung even more frequently in Catholic, Anglican, and Eastern Orthodox services, such as vespers, evening prayers, and Sunday matins. In addition to Johann Sebastian Bach, many composers have set Mary's humble words to magnificent music, including Vivaldi, Anton Bruckner, Rachmaninoff, and Ralph Vaughan Williams. As beautiful as all these musical compositions are, they are like gilded frames around a simply rendered painting. The true artistry and power of the Magnificat is not in the frame but in the lines spoken by the virgin herself.

I wish I could step into a time machine and journey back to that day when young Mary, a girl probably no older than fourteen years old, walked that dusty road into the hills of

Judea to the home of her cousin Elizabeth. I wish I could be there to see Elizabeth and Mary embrace and to hear the words of the Magnificat from Mary's own lips, spoken for the first time in history.

It's true, I wouldn't understand the Aramaic language in which Mary spoke these words. But I wouldn't need to. I would see the joy of the Magnificat shining in her eyes, and I would hear the sweet humility and reverent praise in the delicate vibrations of her voice. What a privilege for Elizabeth to hear this prayer, which would be recited millions of times down through the ages, and to hear it in Mary's songlike voice for the very first time in human history.

> My soul glorifies the Lord
>> and my spirit rejoices in God my Savior,
> for he has been mindful
>> of the humble state of his servant.
> From now on all generations will call me blessed,
>> for the Mighty One has done great things for me—
>> holy is his name.
> His mercy extends to those who fear him,
>> from generation to generation.
> He has performed mighty deeds with his arm;
>> he has scattered those who are proud in their in-
>> most thoughts.
> He has brought down rulers from their thrones
>> but has lifted up the humble.
> He has filled the hungry with good things
>> but has sent the rich away empty.
> He has helped his servant Israel,
>> remembering to be merciful
> to Abraham and his descendants forever,
>> just as he promised our ancestors. (Luke 1:46–55)

Mary composed these words out of a heart full of gratitude. God had chosen to bless her among all women by placing in her womb the baby who would become the Savior of the world. The mystery of the incarnation was growing inside her. The Creator of all creation was implanted as an embryo in the womb of one of His creatures. The most important human life ever conceived was growing inside her. The most important time in history had just begun. The long-promised Messiah would soon be born—and she would be His mother!

How could she not sing? How could she not pray? How could she not praise God for the honor He had given her?

A Role Model for Generations to Come

When I think of this teenage girl and the awesome honor and responsibility that was bestowed on her and the humility and joy with which she received it, I can't help but think about teenagers today. I know so many Christian teenagers who are committed to living for Christ, who often must take bold and courageous stands against bullying peers, anti-Christian school officials, a hostile post-Christian culture, and the entertainment media that seeks to break down their faith and values.

I also think about non-Christian teens growing up in a world that seeks to destroy them. They are immersed in a corrosive cultural philosophy that says they are nothing but evolved animals in a godless and unfeeling universe driven solely by hormones, instincts, and passions. My heart breaks for teenagers who have never heard the good news of Jesus Christ.

The virgin Mary, the mother of Jesus, expresses a pure and godly sense of self-worth, self-esteem, and self-love in the Magnificat. I wish every young person in the world could read or hear her words, learn from her example, and know what it means to be truly loved and blessed by God. I wish they could know that the Son of God came from heaven, died on the cross, and rose again for their salvation. I wish they would receive Him so they could know that He has adopted them as sons and daughters, and has given them a new name, His name, and that He alone can bring them the joy and fulfillment they seek in this life, along with eternal life in heaven.

Mary is a role model—a beautiful teenage example of femininity, inner beauty, spirituality, and strength of character and personality. She faced a crisis that you and I can't fully understand, though we can try to put ourselves in her place. Because of her belief in the Word of God, because of her trust in the promises of God, because of her deep and abiding relationship with God, she faced this crisis with confidence and faith.

In her prayer she says, "From now on all generations will call me blessed" (v. 48), and two thousand years of Christian history have proven her right. Her prayer is a magnificent model that we can study and emulate. This prayer exemplifies the lasting power of authentic, biblical self-esteem and the perfect balance of confidence and humility. The personality of this young teenager was not warped by materialism, corrupted by possessions, or distorted by peer pressure. Her spirit was formed and shaped by a lifetime of immersion in the Word of God.

As you read through the Magnificat of Mary, you may notice echoes of other passages of Scripture in these words. No, Mary does not quote any Old Testament passage verbatim, but you can sense the sacred influence of the books of Moses, the prophets, and especially from the song of Hannah (1 Sam. 2:1–10), which we saw in chapter 2. Mary had undoubtedly spent many hours in the synagogue, listening to the reading and exposition of Old Testament Scripture. That's why these inspired words came so readily to her lips. Her Magnificat is rich in biblical truth and emotional intensity because throughout her brief span of years, she saturated her mind with the powerful insights that are only found in the timeless Word of God.

More than two thousand years ago, this young girl from Nazareth—the least of all the towns of that region—expressed a healthy self-esteem and a humble and selfless spirit. No one can make you feel inferior without your consent, and Mary would give no such consent, even though there were surely many people who wanted to destroy her reputation because she was unwed and pregnant. She said, "My spirit rejoices in God my Savior, for he has been mindful of the humble state of his servant" (vv. 47–48).

It takes a healthy self-esteem to be humble. People with a broken self-esteem, who think themselves inferior, cannot afford to appear humble. They have to let others know how smart they are, how beautiful they are, and how accomplished they are to compensate for their feelings of inferiority and their lack of self-confidence. Only those who are secure in themselves, who are comfortable in their own skin, can afford to take the role of the humble servant.

God chose Mary to play a very difficult part on the world stage and on the stage of history. She carried within her womb the Savior of humanity, conceived miraculously by the Holy Spirit. She had never been with a man, yet she was pregnant. But who would believe that? How could she prove that to anyone?

Mary was a teenage girl in a society where only the word of an adult male mattered. She was a girl living in poverty in a society where only wealth and power mattered. She was unmarried and pregnant in a society where the law said she could be stoned to death for sexual sin. Society had stacked the deck against her, yet she was committed to living obediently to God's Word. She was committed to trusting in the promises of God and to allowing God to use her life for His glory as He would sovereignly see fit. Her faith is an example to us all.

Fulfilling Our Deepest Longings

Today we treat celebrities as gods and goddesses and even call them "idols." The secular media celebrates their blatant immorality, arrogance, and narcissism. But celebrities are here today, gone tomorrow—if not sooner. In her humility and faithfulness, Mary continues to instruct and inspire generations. Over the centuries since this teenage girl spoke this prayer, millions of parents have named their daughters Mary, Marie, Maria, Mariette, Maryam, Moira, or another of the many variations of this beautiful name. Long after the celebrities of our time are forgotten, the name of Mary will still be blessed.

From the primitive tenth-century *Golden Madonna of Essen* to the surrealistic *Madonna of Port Lligat* by Salvador Dalí of the twentieth century, countless artists have imagined Mary as a symbol of feminine innocence, purity, and beauty. We don't know if Mary, the mother of Jesus, was outwardly beautiful or not—but we do know that, at the very least, she possessed the beauty of holiness, the beauty of being surrendered to the Lord, the beauty of desiring to obey God regardless of the cost, and the beauty of being the willing handmaiden of the Lord.

She was favored and blessed by God because of her beautiful, humble, faithful spirit, and what greater beauty could any woman desire than that? As a virtuous and innocent virgin, she was privileged by God to carry His Son. She was honored to be chosen as the mother of the Messiah. Mary humbly and virtuously fulfilled the deepest longings of the human race since God told the serpent in the Garden of Eden:

> And I will put enmity
>> between you and the woman,
>> and between your offspring and hers;
> he will crush your head,
>> and you will strike his heel. (Gen. 3:15)

Why did Jesus have to be born of a virgin? Because the Son of God could not possibly be born by the natural biological process. Had Jesus been conceived by an earthly father, he could not have saved us from our sin. Why? Because he would have been a sinner like us. Only the One who is sinless can pay the price for our sin.

Please don't miss what I am about to tell you: there is a miracle that takes place every time a person comes to Christ, receives Christ as Lord and Savior, and is born again. I don't think we value that miracle nearly as much as we should. Many of us as Christians lose our passion and excitement over that miracle. We take that miracle for granted. We forget what it really means to have Christ born in our lives.

Here's what that miracle means: when Christ is born in our hearts, we too are favored by God.

We are favored by God when Christ comes into our lives.

We are favored by God when He transforms our hearts.

We are favored by God when He changes our eternal destinations.

We are favored by God when He gives us the faith to believe in Him.

We are favored by God when He gives us the gift of the Holy Spirit.

That is all the self-esteem you and I will ever need, even as we live in this hostile and corrosive society. That is all the self-esteem we will need as we face anti-Christian prejudice on our campuses, in the workplace, in the government, and in the marketplace. That is all the self-esteem we will need as we watch the news and see our faith mocked, our Lord despised, and our Christian witness scorned.

No matter what the future holds, no matter how we are persecuted or hunted down because of our faith in Christ, we are favored by God because Christ has been born in our hearts.

Three Distinctive Features of Mary's Prayer

Now let's take a closer look at Mary's prayer of praise. There are three features that immediately attract our attention:

Mary glorifies and magnifies the Lord (vv. 46–47).

Mary praises God for His grace (vv. 48–52).

Mary thanks God for His faithfulness (vv. 53–55).

Mary Glorifies and Magnifies the Lord

First and foremost, Mary magnifies and glorifies the Lord. We must remember that Mary was in a predicament. She was pregnant and unmarried. This sweet, faithful, godly virgin became an outcast in her community as soon as the town gossips noticed her baby bump and their tongues started wagging. So when she says, "My soul glorifies the Lord and my spirit rejoices in God my Savior" (vv. 46–47), she is not rejoicing in her wonderful circumstances, nor is she rejoicing in the close friends who are standing by her at this time, nor is she rejoicing in how pleased and excited her parents are over her pregnancy. (Can you imagine how they reacted to the news?)

No, Mary's soul glorifies the Lord and rejoices in Him because she has placed all her trust in Him and no trust whatsoever in her circumstances. Forsaken by friends and misunderstood by family, she rests in the favor and blessing of her Lord. Her soul, her spirit, her emotions, her mind, and even her body (which is probably becoming somewhat hormonal by this time) are bound up in praising, exalting, and blessing the One who has blessed her with His favor.

You may not feel favored by God right now. As you look at your circumstances, as you take stock of your family relationships and friendships, as you think about your reputation in the community, as you look at your bank statement and your list of assets, as you consider your health and other measures of personal well-being, you may not feel particularly blessed. Don't let your circumstances blind you to the goodness of God. Don't let temporary conditions negatively impact your eternal relationship with God.

Praise Him in the triumphs and in the predicaments. Praise Him in the sunshine and in the shadows. Praise Him when your eyes are sparkling with joy and when they glisten with tears. If you are eternally saved, you are favored by God.

Show me a person whose prayer life is focused on magnifying the Lord, and I will show you a person who is contented and full of joy. Show me a person whose prayer life is consumed with glorifying God, and I will show you a truly happy person. Show me a person whose prayer life is focused on seeking the righteousness of God, and I will show you a truly satisfied Christian.

If anyone in the world would have a right to worry and be anxious and upset, it is this pregnant teenage virgin. Her life was on the line. Her reputation had been trashed. Her honor was called into question. Her future was uncertain. But her response to her circumstances shows us why God selected her, among all the young women in Israel, to be the mother of the Messiah. Regardless of her circumstances, she glorified and magnified the name of the Lord.

Mary Praises God for His Grace

There is a pattern in Mary's prayer that points to the grace of God. In verse 48 she says, "For he has been mindful of the humble state of his servant. From now on all generations will call me blessed." Mary saw herself as merely a humble servant of God, an instrument in the hand of God.

God always favors the humble. My friend John Ashcroft, who was the governor of Missouri, then a US Senator, then Attorney General of the United States in the George W. Bush administration, told about a lesson in humility he learned from his father.

A few months after his father's death, Ashcroft was at an airport, trying to board a delayed flight bound for Washington, with a connection in St. Louis. The ticket agent wouldn't let him board. "You won't make your connection," the agent insisted. "I'm going to put you on a later flight." Ashcroft didn't want to take the later plane, which would arrive in Washington at midnight, so he argued with the agent. The agent, however, wouldn't budge. He insisted on changing the ticket, which only frustrated and angered Ashcroft all the more.

Then, from the back of the line, Ashcroft heard someone say, "Yeah, he thinks he can do anything because he's a senator."

When he heard that biting remark, Ashcroft recalled something his late father once said to him: "Someday, I hope someone will come up to you and say, 'Senator, your spirit is showing.'" That day had come, and John Ashcroft realized he was showing a spirit of arrogance, not a spirit of godly humility.

"I thought of all my father had taught me," Ashcroft later reflected. "Now that he was dead, I felt a new urgency to personify the principles he had held so dear. Yet in times like these, I was a poor representative at best."

He later apologized to the ticket agent. "I knew I needed to ask forgiveness," he said, "for my arrogant spirit."[1]

Political power often inflates the egos of those who wield it. By contrast, Mary, the mother of Jesus, exemplifies a spirit of humility in her prayer. John Ashcroft rediscovered his own spirit of humility just in time. There are many other people in politics, in business, and yes, in the church, who could learn an important lesson from this humble teenage girl.

The secret of Mary's courage and strength in the face of these difficult circumstances was *the grace of God*. Mary was conscious of the grace of God, the favor of God, and the mercy of God, so she kept her head up in spite of the whispering of the town gossips and the muttering of the religious leaders who might decide at any moment to cast the first stone.

Once, when Jesus described his cousin John the Baptist, he said, "I tell you, among those born of women there is no one greater than John" (Luke 7:28). Why did Jesus say that? Because John the Baptist's motto was "He must become greater; I must become less" (John 3:30). John the Baptist had the same humble spirit that Mary demonstrates in the Magnificat. Mary's greatness was in her humility, and she focused her prayer life on the grace of God.

In verses 51–52 Mary says, "He has performed mighty deeds with his arm; he has scattered those who are proud in their inmost thoughts. He has brought down rulers from their thrones but has lifted up the humble." Prideful, arrogant people come and go. They will continue to come and go. From Nebuchadnezzar of Babylon to Alexander the Great, from the Caesars of Rome to the Czars of Russia, from Hitler and Mussolini to Saddam Hussein and Muammar Gaddafi, arrogant men rise to the pinnacle of power, then fall to destruction and doom.

And yet, after two thousand years, a humble teenage virgin is still praised for her obedience, still emulated for her faith, still blessed for her virtue. I love the way God stands history on its head. In the first century, at the height of the Roman Empire, Caesar was everything and the apostle Paul was nothing. But today, we name our children Paul—and we name our dogs Caesar.

God gives grace to the humble, and God humbles the proud.

Mary Thanks God for His Faithfulness

Third, let's see how Mary thanked God for His faithfulness. You cannot read the Bible without noting that God has been faithful to all His promises. Even when His people became impatient and accused Him of unfaithfulness, He steadfastly kept *all* His promises. That is what Mary is saying in the closing lines of the Magnificat: "He has filled the hungry with good things but has sent the rich away empty. He has helped his servant Israel, remembering to be merciful to Abraham and his descendants forever, just as he promised our ancestors" (vv. 53–55).

God promised Abraham and Sarah a son. Twenty-five years later, He delivered on His promise. He promised to deliver His people from Egyptian bondage. Four centuries later, He did. He promised Moses that He would take the people of Israel into the promised land. Four decades later, He did. Century after century, from Genesis through Malachi, God promised to send the Messiah. In the fullness of time, in accordance with His promise, Jesus was born of a virgin.

Mary, who embodied and personified God's fulfilled promise to the human race, was saying through the Magnificat, "God always keeps His promises."

Are you willing to trust Him to keep His promises to you?
Are you willing to magnify and glorify His name above all else?
Are you willing to bear witness to His grace, His mercy, and His faithfulness?

Glorify God in all circumstances. Magnify His name at all times. That is the essence of the prayer of Mary, the mother of our Savior.

That is the key to power in prayer.

Epilogue
The Purpose of Prayer

Rodney "Gipsy" Smith (1860–1947) was a British evangelist and an early missionary worker in the Salvation Army. He was nicknamed Gipsy because he was born in a lean-to tent in a Romani (Gypsy) camp in Epping Forest near London. At one of his evangelistic meetings, a man asked him the secret of revival. Gipsy Smith replied, "Go home and take a piece of chalk. Draw a circle around yourself. Then pray, 'O Lord, revive everything inside this circle.'"[1]

Gipsy Smith understood that the purpose of prayer is not to change God but to allow God to change us. The purpose of prayer is to bring God's power into our lives, to open us up to God's blessings and God's power to change us.

But that's not how we tend to pray, is it? We pray to persuade God, to coax Him into seeing our point of view. We pray to inform God of a situation or a need that we think He clearly doesn't know about. Or we pray to manipulate God into giving us what we want or what we think we need.

But as we have seen again and again throughout this book, the real purpose of prayer is to get us on our knees, with our heads bowed and our hearts surrendered to God and His will.

If we fail to understand God's purpose for prayer, we will continue to pray for the wrong things, with the wrong attitude, with the wrong results, and we will miss the many blessings God wants to shower on our lives. So please understand this all-important principle: *the real purpose of prayer is to allow God to be glorified and magnified in our lives.* Yes, God has also given us the right and the power and the ability to pray for our needs to be met. He meets our needs through prayer because He loves us. And yet, when God meets our needs through prayer, He gets the glory.

So it all comes down to glorifying and magnifying God.

Jesus told His disciples, "And I will do whatever you ask in my name, so that the Father may be glorified in the Son. You may ask me for anything in my name, and I will do it" (John 14:13–14). I have heard some very bad theology based on these verses. I have heard people suggest that Jesus has given us a blank check; all we have to do is sign His name to it, and anything we ask for is ours. Some people think that praying in the name of Jesus simply means to add the words *In Jesus's name, amen* at the end of our prayers.

No! To pray in the name of Jesus is to pray for the things that will bring glory and honor to the name of Jesus. If we pray that God will be glorified in our lives, that is praying in the name of Jesus. If we pray that many people would come to know Jesus through our witness, that is praying in the name of Jesus. If we tell Jesus He would be glorified if we had a $2 million Aston Martin car, a country club membership, and a mansion on the bluffs, that is *not* praying in the name of Jesus. That is praying in our own name.

Some people teach that if we pray with enough faith or enough emotional fervor, or pray in just the right way with just the right words, God will magically give us whatever we ask for. A few moments' reflection shows how ridiculous that notion is. Prayer is not a slot machine in which we hope to hit the right combination and win the jackpot.

Does a loving father give his children everything they ask for? Of course not. If you love your children, you sometimes tell them "No," or perhaps, "Not right now." When my children were small, they asked for all kinds of things. They asked for ice cream and cake for breakfast. They asked to stay up all night. They asked for all the glittering toys they saw advertised on TV. As loving parents, my wife and I often said no to their requests. They thought we were being unfair, but we knew best. And God, our heavenly Father, knows what is best for us. He gives good gifts to those who ask Him (Matt. 7:11; Luke 11:13), and sometimes, in His great love for us, He says no to our prayers.

Jesus taught us by His example that prayer is a discipline. That means it takes effort and commitment to build a habit of prayer. Jesus didn't tell us that we have to pray at any particular time, but He did set an example of rising early in the morning, going off to a secluded place, and spending time alone with God the Father every day. Prayer is a conversation between God the Father and His children. It's a dialogue, not a monologue. Part of praying, then, is listening. Part of praying is sitting quietly and clearing our thoughts and waiting for the still, small voice of God's Spirit. What kind of conversation are you having with God if you do all the talking?

In addition to a daily and regular discipline of prayer, we are commanded in Scripture to pray continually, to pray anywhere and everywhere, to pray in every circumstance and at every opportunity. Prayer—talking to God the Father—is not just asking God for what we want. Prayer is a way of life—literally, a way of sustaining our spiritual life, of staying spiritually alive. It's the spiritual equivalent of breathing. We pray continuously, breathing in and breathing out, speaking and listening, in a constant awareness of God's presence.

Prayer is probably the most amazing thing we ever do. Think about it: the Creator of the universe, the One who created time and space, heaven and earth, and all living creatures, invites you and me into His presence for fellowship. He says to us, "Come to Me any time with any question, any concern, any need. I am always here, I am always listening, I am always available. What would you like to talk about today?"

In Matthew 6 Jesus gave us a pattern for prayer, which we call the Lord's Prayer. Jesus says:

> This, then, is how you should pray:
>
> "Our Father in heaven,
> hallowed be your name,
> your kingdom come,
> your will be done,
>   on earth as it is in heaven.
> Give us today our daily bread.
> And forgive us our debts,
>   as we also have forgiven our debtors.
> And lead us not into temptation,
>   but deliver us from the evil one." (Matt. 6:9–13)

It's fine to memorize and recite the Lord's Prayer, but let us not simply rattle off the words without sincerely and passionately meaning them. Remember that Jesus warned His followers not to pray as the Pharisees prayed, with meaningless repetition. Let's make sure we don't turn the Lord's Prayer into just another Pharisee's prayer. Let's pray this prayer from the depths of our heart in all sincerity.

When we pray, "Hallowed be your name," let's pray from our hearts that God's name would be glorified and magnified. When we pray, "Your will be done, on earth as it is in heaven," let's pray in absolute submission to God's sovereign will. When we pray, "And forgive us our debts, as we also have forgiven our debtors," let's think carefully about those who have wronged us, as well as those we have wronged, and make sure that we forgive and ask for forgiveness. And when we pray, "And lead us not into temptation, but deliver us from the evil one," let's sincerely ask God to give us victory over temptation and sin. In times of temptation, let's pray this prayer again and again for as long as it takes to send Satan fleeing from us and to break the grip of sin in our lives. Let's allow this prayer to impact our lives and change us for the glory of God.

The seven people I have profiled in this book were ordinary people who experienced an extraordinary relationship with God through prayer. There is nothing about the prayer life of Eliezer, Hannah, David, Daniel, Jonah, Habakkuk, or Mary that is beyond our ability to achieve. These individuals were not spiritual superheroes. They were ordinary people whose lives were transformed by the quantity of time they spent in fellowship with our awesome and amazing God.

Now that you have read this book, you may want to go back to the beginning and reread each of these prayers. This book has seven chapters—one for each day of the week. Why not spend a week in this book, immersing your heart and mind in these prayers? Ask God to teach you, change you, and transform your prayer life through the extraordinary prayers of these ordinary people of the Bible.

Friend in Christ, I am praying for you as you apply these biblical insights to your daily walk with God. May God bless you and impact your life in a powerful way as you walk and talk with Him each day.

Notes

Introduction

1. Harold Melvin Stanford, ed., *The Standard Reference Work: For the Home, School and Library*, vol. 10 (Minneapolis: Standard Education Society, 1922), 306.

Chapter 1 Eliezer

1. Yogi Berra with Dave Kaplan, *When You Come to a Fork in the Road, Take It! Inspiration and Wisdom from One of Baseball's Greatest Heroes* (New York: Hyperion, 2001), 1.

2. Quoted in Donald Grey Barnhouse, *First Things First* (Philadelphia: The Bible Study Hour, 1961), 17.

3. Robert Irwin, *Camel* (London: Reaktion Books, 2010), 19; Murray E. Fowler, "Blood Cells Protect from Dehydration: Dromedary," AskNature .org, August 10, 2010, https://asknature.org/strategy/blood-cells-protect -from-dehydration/.

4. J. M. Foster, "The Wonderful Love of Christ," *The Reformed Presbyterian and Covenanter*, January 1883 (Pittsburgh: Myers, Shinkle & Co., 1883), 137.

Chapter 2 Hannah

1. Rupert Hughes, "When Will Rogers Wept," *Rockland Journal News*, November 4, 1935, 2.

2. Sisley Huddleston, *Paris Salons, Cafés, Studios* (New York: Lippincott, 1928), 134.

Chapter 3 David

1. Charles Haddon Spurgeon, *The Treasury of David*, vol. 3 (New York: Funk & Wagnalls, 1882), 421.

2. John Coates, "Write a Letter to Terrorists! Children Told to 'Respect' Killers in New Teaching Aid," *Express*, May 28, 2017, http://www.express.co.uk/news/uk/810115/school-children-told-respect-killers-teaching-aid-talking-about-terrorism; Virginia Hale, "UK Children Taught to 'Respect' Terrorists Who Kill over 'Unfair' Treatment," Breitbart.com, May 30, 2017, http://www.breitbart.com/london/2017/05/30/teaching-terror-children-respect-killers/.

3. Jeffrey Salkin, "I was Maimonides' Ghostwriter (and Other Alternative Facts)," RNS, January 23, 2017, http://religionnews.com/2017/01/23/alternative-facts/.

Chapter 4 Daniel

1. Todd Starnes, "Court Rules High School Football Coach Cannot Pray on the Field," FoxNews.com, August 23, 2017, http://www.foxnews.com/opinion/2017/08/23/court-rules-high-school-football-coach-cannot-pray-on-field.html; Maura Dolan, "Football Coach's On-Field Prayer Not Protected by Constitution, Appeals Court Rules," *Los Angeles Times*, August 23, 2017, http://www.latimes.com/nation/la-na-football-coach-prayer-20170823-story.html.

2. Quoted in Timothy Keller, *Prayer: Experiencing Awe and Intimacy with God* (New York: Dutton, 2014), 22.

Chapter 5 Jonah

1. Nick Bilton, "Steve Jobs Was a Low-Tech Parent," *New York Times*, September 10, 2014, https://www.nytimes.com/2014/09/11/fashion/steve-jobs-apple-was-a-low-tech-parent.html.

2. Monica Mark, "Nigerian Sailor 'a Phenomenon' for Surviving in Air Pocket for 60 Hours," *The Guardian*, June 12, 2013, https://www.theguardian.com/world/2013/jun/12/nigeria-sailor-survive-air-pocket; Associated Press, "Raw: Divers Find Man Alive in Sunken Tugboat," YouTube.com, December 3, 2013, https://www.youtube.com/watch?v=ArWGILmKCqE&feature=youtu.be; Marc Lallanilla, "Here's How That Cook Survived inside Sunken Ship for Three Days," HuffingtonPost.com, January 23, 2014, https://www.huffingtonpost.com/2013/12/05/cook-survived-sunken-ship-three-days_n_4391872.html.

Chapter 6 Habakkuk

1. Quoted in Keller, *Prayer*, 106–7.

Chapter 7 Mary

1. John Ashcroft with Gary Thomas, *Lessons from a Father to His Son* (Nashville: Thomas Nelson, 1998), Kindle.

Epilogue

1. David R. Mains, *What's Wrong with Lukewarm?* (Elgin, IL: David C. Cook, 1987), 18.

Michael Youssef is the founder and president of Leading The Way with Dr. Michael Youssef (www.LTW.org), a worldwide ministry that leads the way for people living in spiritual darkness to discover the light of Christ through the creative use of media and on-the-ground ministry teams. His weekly television programs and daily radio programs are broadcast in twenty-five languages and seen worldwide, airing more than twelve thousand times per week. He is also the founding pastor of The Church of The Apostles in Atlanta, Georgia, which has more than three thousand members. Youssef was born in Egypt and lived in Lebanon and Australia before coming to the United States. In 1984, he fulfilled a childhood dream of becoming an American citizen. He holds degrees from Moore College in Sydney, Australia, and Fuller Theological Seminary in California. In 1984, he earned a PhD in social anthropology from Emory University. He and his wife live in Atlanta and have four grown children and eight grandchildren.

Connect with

Dr. Michael Youssef!

Follow Dr. Youssef for life-giving truth, behind-the-scenes ministry updates, and much more.

MichaelYoussef.com

Biblical Encouragement
for You—Anytime, Anywhere

Leading The Way with Dr. Michael Youssef is passionately proclaiming uncompromising Truth through every major form of media, empowering you to know and follow Christ. There are many FREE ways you can connect with Dr. Youssef's teachings:

- Thousands of sermons and articles online
- TV and radio programs worldwide
- Apps for your phone or tablet
- A monthly magazine, and more!

Learn more at **LTW.org/Connect**

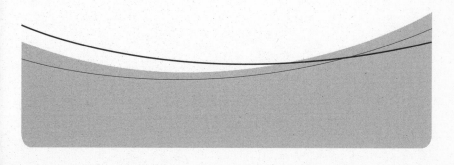